SCHOLASTIC

AF644758

# SCHOLASTIC GO GRAMMAR

## Course Book

Level 5

Copyright © Blake Education 2008

Additional material © Scholastic India Pvt Ltd 2008

Additional illustrations by Durgadatt Pandey

Cover design by Priya Kuriyan

All rights reserved.

Published by Scholastic India Pvt. Ltd.
A subsidiary of Scholastic Inc., New York, 10012 (USA).
*Publishers since 1920,* with international operations in Canada, Australia, New Zealand,
the United Kingdom, India, and Hong Kong.

No part of this publication may be reproduced in whole or in part, or stored in a retrieval system, or transmitted in any form or by any means, electronic, mechanical, photocopying, recording, or otherwise without the written permission of the publisher.

For information regarding permission, write to:
Scholastic India Pvt. Ltd.
A-27, Ground Floor, Bharti Sigma Centre
Infocity-1, Sector 34, Gurgaon (Haryana) 122001
Email: info_in@scholastic.asia

Typeset at Digital Expressions

First edition: 2008
Reprinted: 2009 (thrice), 2010 (twice), 2011 (four times), 2012 (thrice), 2013 (twice), 2014 (twice),
2015 (twice), 2016 (thrice), 2017 (twice), 2018 (twice), 2019 (twice), 2020, 2021, 2023 (twice),
2024, 2025

ISBN-13: 978-81-8477-148-0

# Contents

# Thank You!

**The *Go Grammar* books were sent out to approximately eighty schools across the country for primary school principals, departmental heads and teachers to give their feedback on the contents.**
**The publishers would like to thank all those who took the time out of their busy schedules to go through the books and make many valuable suggestions, which have been duly incorporated.**

Alaukika Khachar, The Rajkumar College, Rajkot
Alka Kshetrapal, Delhi Public School, Bilaspur
Anjana Henry, Delhi Public School, Bilaspur
Anuradha Tandan, Seth Anandram Jaipuria School, Kanpur
Arpita Mitra, Delhi Public School, Bilaspur
Caroline O Conner, Delhi Public School, Bilaspur
Denise Wesley, Delhi Public School, Bilaspur
G. Annapurna, Delhi Public School, Bilaspur
Hemavathi, N.S.N Matric Hr Sec School, Chennai
Indrani Ganguly, St. John's Whitehall Secondary School, Shillong
Madhu Hora, Seth Anandram Jaipuria School, Kanpur
Manisha Francis, Delhi Public School, Bilaspur
Manju Negi, R.D. Rajpal Public School, New Delhi
Manu Mishra, Delhi Public School, Bilaspur
Mathew Panamkat, Doon Public School, Delhi
Maushumi Deb, St. John's Whitehall Secondary School, Shillong
Maya Shukla, Delhi Public School, Bilaspur
Monisha Bhattacharya, Julien Day School, Kolkata
N. Sambasivarao, Pragathi Vidya Niketan, Hyderabad
Neha Jain, Gyan Bharati School, New Delhi
P. Nirmala, Delhi Public School, Vishakapatnam
Payal Dubey, Seth Anandram Jaipuria School, Kanpur
R. Niranjani, Chinmaya Vidyalaya, Anna Nagar, Chennai
Radhika Wadhwa, Gyan Bharati School, New Delhi
Renu Vashishta, Maharana Mewar Vidya Mandir, Udaipur
Renuka Semwal, Gyan Bharati School, New Delhi
Reshmi Sarkar, R.D. Rajpal Public School, New Delhi
S. Haldia, MGD Girls School, Jaipur
Sagarika Satpathy, Delhi Public School, Vishakapatnam
Sandeep Mishra, Delhi Public School, Bilaspur
Sangeeta Bali, R.D. Rajpal Public School, New Delhi
Shobha Gopakumar, Delhi Public School, Vishakapatnam
Sonia Abraham, Delhi Public School, Bilaspur
Sujatha, N.S.N Matric Hr Sec School, Chennai
Sulekha Bhattacharya, St. John's Whitehall Secondary School, Shillong
The English Department Co-ordinator, Delhi Public School, Dwarka, New Delhi
Usha Sankar, N.S.N Matric Hr Sec School, Chennai
Vandana Pathak, Delhi Public School, Vishakapatnam
Vasanti Tank, The Rajkumar College, Rajkot

**Special thanks to Sunita Malkani for her assistance and advice.**

**In addition to the people listed above, there were many teachers who did not want their help to be publicly acknowledged. In deference to their wishes, we have not included their names, but we would once again like to acknowledge their valuable help.**

# Introduction

*Go Grammar* is a series of English grammar course books for the primary classes. The books have been created by a panel of eminent authors, school and college teachers, and experienced children's publishers. They have been vetted by school teachers and principals from different parts of India. The approach follows the current NCERT curriculum and pedagogical principles.

Grammar is the heart and soul of language. An understanding of grammar gives mastery and control over all forms of communication, both verbal and written. Students need to develop the skills to express themselves creatively and meaningfully. These books are intended to help students build a strong and solid foundation in language usage.

The *Go Grammar* books cover the following topics:

- Nouns
- Adjectives
- Verbs
- Adverbs
- Tenses
- Prepositions
- Articles
- Conjunctions
- Sentences

For in-depth understanding of the concepts, the book includes the following features:

Read with Your Teacher: This section introduces each topic, giving definitions and examples. With every successive level, it recapitulates what has been taught before and introduces more complex details. Teachers can either choose to start by reading this section with their students when beginning a new topic, or use it as a revision exercise after the chapter has been completed.

Games: The Read with Your Teacher section also includes individual and team activities to reinforce the concepts in a fun manner and to give the students essential verbal practice.

Worksheets: The concepts learnt can be further strengthened through exercise sheets which can be worked on at school or at home. The fun activities and attractive illustrations engage the students' attention and enhance the learning experience.

Composition: This section helps students improve their writing skills. The activities are designed to encourage students to use grammatically correct language. Writing notices, diary entries, messages, paragraphs, book reviews, letters and notes gives students the confidence to use the language effectively and practically.

Revision tests: This thoughtfully planned section helps the students review and evaluate their progress on the concepts they have learnt.

Word banks: The extensive lists of antonyms, homophones, compound words, collective nouns, suffixes and prefixes help improve vocabulary and reinforce the learning.

An informative and motivating set of books, *Go Grammar* will help students apply the rules of grammar in spoken and written English, to make them effective and articulate communicators.

# Nouns

Nouns are words that name people, places, animals and things in a sentence.
Different nouns have different jobs to do.

**Common nouns** name everyday things around us.
**Proper nouns** give people, places, objects and events their given or special names.

**Singular nouns** name one thing.
**Plural nouns** name more than one thing.
Most plural nouns are formed by adding **s** or **es** to the singular noun.
Some plurals are formed by changing the vowels or adding **en.**
For example: foot-feet, man-men, child-children
Some nouns are both singular and plural.
For example: sheep, fish, deer
Some nouns are only plural.
For example: trousers, scissors, cutlery, crockery

## Gender nouns

You have learnt about masculine and feminine nouns. The common gender is names of people that can be either male or female.
For example: writer, doctor.
The neuter gender is when a noun is neither male nor female.
For example: table, chair

**Compound nouns** are made by joining two words together.
For example: snowflake, heartbeat, tablecloth, sandcastle, penknife, butterscotch, basketball
**Possessive nouns** show ownership. An apostrophe is always used.
For example: Jack's horse; the teacher's book; the cats' whiskers
**Collective nouns** are names given to groups of persons or things.
For example: flock (of birds); herd (of cows); crowd (of people)

# Nouns

## Concrete and abstract nouns

A **concrete noun** names a person, animal, place or thing that you can actually see, touch, taste, hear or smell.

**Abstract nouns** deal with things we cannot see, hear, smell or touch. An abstract noun names an idea, a feeling, a quality or an action.
For example: bravery, wisdom, youth, courage, affection

## Countable and Uncountable Nouns

**Countable nouns** are things that we can count.
For example: pencil. We can count pencils. We can have one, two, three or more pencils.
Countable nouns can be singular or plural. We can use **a few** and **many** with countable nouns.
For example: I've got a few dollars. I haven't got many eggs.
**People** is a countable noun. **People** is the plural of person and we can count persons.
**Uncountable nouns** are items or concepts that we cannot divide into separate elements. We cannot count them.
For example: we cannot count **water**. We can count **bottles of water** or **litres of water**, but we cannot count water itself. Examples of uncountable nouns are music, furniture, luggage, sugar, gas, money.
We usually treat uncountable nouns as singular.
For example: The furniture is made of teak wood.
We can use some, any, a little and much with uncountable nouns.

**Verbal nouns** are present participles used as nouns.
For example: Skiing is a winter sport. Let's go bowling. Seeing is believing.

## Noun groups

A noun group is a group of words built around a noun.
For example: one chocolate cake, my straw hat, a tiny, black spider

WORK SHEET 1

# Nouns

**Nouns can be common or proper, singular or plural, masculine, feminine or neuter, concrete or abstract, countable or uncountable, collective or compound.**

**1 Circle the first letter of each noun in the following sports report. Then write these letters to make the names of three sports.**

Heroes against Odds

The crowd screamed for Kyle Ellis as the youngster led his team, The Eagles, to win the nationals in Newport. An invitation to play soccer here had been hard to get. But the team set a record for young athletes. And they won the championship because of Kyle.

Sports *a* ___ ___ ___ ___ ___ ___

*b* ___ ___ ___ ___ ___ ___

*c* ___ ___ ___ ___ ___

**2 Change the underlined nouns to plurals.**

*a* We saw many fox in the forest. __________

*b* My tooth is broken. __________

*c* The child passed the ball through the ring. __________ __________ __________

*d* The plate is dirty. __________

*e* Go through the gate. __________

*f* The strawberry was very sweet. __________

*g* My brother's team won the match. __________

**3 Change the following into possessive nouns.**

coaches __________

boys __________

children __________

referee __________

family __________

foxes __________

buffalo __________

schools __________

WORK SHEET 2

# Nouns

**Nouns name people, places, animals, feelings and the everyday things around us.**

**1 Use apostrophes to show ownership.**

*a* I heard the umpire whistle.

______________________________

*b* I look after my family pets.

______________________________

*c* Birds wings beat in the darkening sky.

______________________________

*d* They will soon know the voters preferences.

______________________________

*e* There are hundreds of sheep on my aunt and uncle farm.

______________________________

**2 Add the missing nouns in the following story.**

Give the story a title.

______________________________

Once a sly, mean fox invited a stork to dinner. The fox though he would play a __________ on the stork. The only ___________ he served was some thin soup in a shallow _________. The fox lapped up his own soup very quickly. Because the stork had a long, thin __________, she could not lap up even a mouthful. At the end of the ___________, the stork was still hungry. "What a pity, my ___________ that you are not hungry. The ____________ was very tasty!"

# Nouns

**Nouns name people, places, animals, feelings and the everyday things around us.**

**1 Circle the abstract nouns in the following sentences.**

*a* In great excitement, the children opened their Christmas presents.

*b* As the storm raged around us, we gave up all hope of saving our boat.

*c* My grandfather is a man of great wisdom.

*d* He found it hard to accept the criticism of his coach.

*e* With great determination, Kara completed the marathon.

**2 Match the collective nouns with the animals they are used for.**

| | |
|---|---|
| shoal | owls |
| flock | wolves |
| gaggle | chickens |
| herd | bees |
| murder | frogs |
| swarm | geese |
| army | buffalo |
| pack | birds |
| parliament | crows |
| pride | fish |
| brood | lions |

**3 Write six compound words using the following words. (Words can be used more than once.)**

| | | | | | | |
|---|---|---|---|---|---|---|
| day | junk | house | water | farm | side | sun |
| yard | time | light | life | back | play | line |

______________ ______________ ______________

______________ ______________ ______________

WORK SHEET 4

# Nouns

**Nouns name people, places, animals, feelings and the everyday things around us.**

**1 Write the plural form of the following nouns.**

church ______ chief ______ chimney ______ invention ______ lullaby ______

**2 The gender nouns are all mixed up. Write the matching pairs.**

| | | | | | | | |
|---|---|---|---|---|---|---|---|
| bull | mother | waitress | stallion | madam | rooster | poet | hen |
| bitch | dog | cow | poetess | father | mare | sir | waiter |

______ ______ ______ ______

______ ______ ______ ______

______ ______ ______ ______

______ ______ ______ ______

# Nouns

**Nouns name people, places, animals, feelings and the everyday things around us.**

**1 Highlight the nouns in this nursery rhyme.**

There was a crooked man who had a crooked smile.
He found a crooked sixpence upon a crooked stile.
He bought a crooked cat that had a crooked mouse
And they all lived together in a little crooked house.

*CHECK... Does this word name something?*

**2 Now try spotting the nine nouns in this extract from the poem, 'Killarney'.**

Killarney's hills are purple still
In shadowed mists they lie
Till dawn creeps in with fingers chill
And the magpie's wakening cry
Stirs the echoes in the sleeping valley.

**3 Write a two-line poem of your own, using only nouns.**
**The last two nouns should rhyme.**
**Choose any topic such as sport, shops, toys or clothes.**
**Here is one called 'Breakfast'.**

*Breakfast*
*Bread, butter, eggs, ham*
*Sausages, tea, toast, jam.*

______________________________
______________________________
______________________________

**4 Alliteration is a language device where a number of words in a row begin with the same letter, such as *pork pies* or *sizzling sausages*.**
**Alliteration makes language rich and colourful, and appeals to the ear of the listener.**
**Complete these word pairs by adding a noun beginning with the same letter.**

| | | | |
|---|---|---|---|
| broken ________ | slippery ________ | rough ________ | happy ________ |
| terrible ________ | fantastic ________ | dirty ________ | bony ________ |
| sleepy ________ | plump ________ | mighty ________ | heavy ________ |
| creamy ________ | baggy ________ | bizarre ________ | errant ________ |

WORK SHEET 6

# Abstract Nouns

**Abstract ideas are often explained through metaphors. For example:** Sadness is the lonely cry of a seagull. Happiness is running barefoot in the rain.

Some other examples: **Embarrassment** is a red face and shaky knees.
**Fear** is the thunder of a beating heart.
**Comfort** is hot chocolate at bedtime.
**Love** is the joy of a bird in flight.

**Write a poem, design a sign, or compose a greeting card to define an abstract idea or feeling. Choose one of these, or choose one of your own.**

*trust friendship happiness disappointment sadness love excitement*

# Noun Phrases

**Noun phrases do the same work as nouns. For example:**
Walking every day is good exercise. I like climbing trees.

Noun phrases can be the **subject** of a sentence, for example: *Playing the piano* is great fun. Noun phrases can be the **object** of a sentence, for example: I like *walking my dog*.

## 1 Highlight the noun phrases in these sentences.

*a* We wanted to go swimming on Sunday.

*b* Being school captain was her greatest dream.

*c* Seeing you there was such a surprise.

*d* We must learn to care for each other.

*e* Riding skateboards is not allowed here!

## 2 Select a noun phrase to complete each sentence.

| | | |
|---|---|---|
| *climbing Mt Everest* | *to fly solo* | *leaving all my friends* |
| *to get home* | *growing orchids* | *waiting patiently* |

*a* Mr Gupta enjoys ______________________________ in his greenhouse.

*b* ______________________________ was really sad.

*c* Jayant wanted ______________________________ before nightfall.

*d* ______________________________ is hard when you are really excited.

*e* ______________________________ was Sir Edmund Hilary's greatest achievement.

*f* Seema's dream was ______________________________ across the Arabian Sea.

## 3 Write four sentences using these noun phrases:

*playing the violin   eating popcorn   to sing a song   flying kites*

______________________________________________________________

______________________________________________________________

______________________________________________________________

______________________________________________________________

WORK SHEET 8

# Verbal Nouns

**Some forms of the verb* can be used as nouns. They are called verbal nouns. They end in –ing.**
**For example:** Walking is good exercise. I enjoy swimming in summer.

**These are present participles doing the work of a noun.*

**1 Underline the verbal nouns.**

*a* A constant buzzing could be heard coming from the laboratory.

*b* Cricket is a favourite Indian sport.

*c* Jatin enjoys bike riding, but Paul prefers skateboarding.

*d* I don't approve of the hunting and shooting of wild animals.

*e* Stargazing is a fascinating hobby.

**2 Join the two parts to complete the sentences. Underline the verbal nouns.**

| | |
|---|---|
| *a* The sheep were frightened | is dangerous. |
| *b* River rafting requires | woke me from my sleep. |
| *c* We heard the croaking of frogs | by the howling of wolves. |
| *d* Playing on the street | a lot of skill and training. |
| *e* The baby's crying | in the waterhole. |

**3 Highlight the verbal nouns in these sentences.**

*a* Trekking is my favourite pastime. During the last holidays, I walked through the lovely valleys of the eastern ranges. All was hushed and quiet. The only sounds I heard were the soft rustlings of leaves, the humming of insects, the chiming of bellbirds and the occasional croaking of green tree frogs.

*b* Waiting for the storm to hit was scary. The wind started with a soft murmuring, which soon grew to a terrible roar. The constant screaming of the wind soon filled our ears and rattled the windows. Then there was the unmistakable cracking of branches being broken by the storm's fury. In horror we watched as the fierce wind tore the roofing off the shed. The whistling and whining of the wind seemed to go on for a very long time. Gradually it died down to a low moan, followed by a deathly silence. The storm had finally passed.

# Verbal Nouns

**Some forms of a verb can be used as a noun. These are called verbal nouns. They end in –ing. For example:** Walking is good exercise. Hurling is an Irish sport.

## 1 Box the verbal noun in each sentence.

*a* My brother is studying for his exams.

*b* My friend does kickboxing.

*c* My uncle sometimes takes me birdwatching.

*d* Driving the car makes my father happy.

*e* Pruning roses is usually done in autumn.

## 2 Join these sentences.

| | |
|---|---|
| *a* Reading | of paper folding. |
| *b* You will need special boots | for stamp collecting. |
| *c* Mum put seasoning | is my favourite pastime. |
| *d* Origami is the art | to go rock climbing. |
| *e* Tom has a large album | in the meat curry. |

## 3 Write the correct verbal nouns in the empty boxes. Add any capital letters that are needed.

*a* [ ] is difficult in the centre of the city.

*b* [ ] on the street is dangerous.

*c* The sport of [ ] began in France.

*d* My grandma loves [ ] .

*e* There is not enough [ ] in our street.

fencing | playing | lighting | parking | knitting

WORK SHEET 10

# Noun Groups

**A group of words built around a noun is called a noun group. They more clearly identify the 'things' we want to speak and write about. For example:** a clock, a grandfather clock, the clock in my bedroom, an old, wind-up clock.

## 1 Complete the noun groups with nouns of your own choice.

the long and dusty ____________

a brown, leather ____________

our favourite ____________

a quiet and peaceful ____________

an isolated, country ____________

a wet and windy ____________

a new, multicoloured ____________

an old and wise ____________

## 2 Select three of the noun groups above. Build sentences around them.

______________________________________________

______________________________________________

______________________________________________

## 3 Use the ideas listed below to form a noun group.

For example: cave, *damp, dark, underground* = the dark and damp underground cave

book, *old, faded, leather* = an old book with faded leather binding

*a* day, windy, wet, cold ____________

*b* dress, red, new, pretty ____________

*c* bike, old, rusty, blue ____________

*d* explorers, brave, adventurous ____________

*e* rocks, granite, rough, grey ____________

## 4 Box the noun groups in these sentences.

*a* Class 7 watched an interesting television programme about global warming.

*b* A white, shining angel was placed on top of the green Christmas tree.

*c* A mean, old fox was prowling around the farmer's henhouse.

*d* A family of sparrows lives in a shady tree in our garden.

# Adjectives

Adjectives are words that give colour, shape, size, sound and feeling to nouns. They paint a clearer picture of the nouns.

**Adjectives of degree** may describe nouns as they are (positive degree)
For example: I have a long rope,
or compared to another (comparative degree)
For example: My rope is longer than yours,
Or compared to all others (superlative degree)
For example: Todd has the longest rope of all.

- Suffixes **–er** and **–est** are usually used to make adjectives of degree. Some adjectives add **–er** or **–est** without any change in their spellings.
  For example: old, older, oldest
  sweet, sweeter, sweetest
- Adjectives that end in **–e** drop the **–e** when adding **–er** or **–est.**
  For example: large, larger, largest

Other adjectives of degree are formed by placing **more** or **most** before the adjective.
**More** and **most** are used before adjectives that already end in a suffix.
For example: beautiful, more beautiful, most beautiful
Helpful, more helpful, most helpful

### Types of adjectives:

**Quantitative adjectives:** these adjectives tell us about the quantity of the noun—how much.

1. I have some money.
2. He has a few coins.
3. The teacher has to correct forty books in the class.

Such adjectives are also called **numeral adjectives.** Sentence 3 is an example of a **definite numeral adjective** whereas sentences 1 and 2 are examples of **indefinite numeral adjectives.**
But both answer the question—how much?
The definite numeral adjectives are of three kinds:
**Cardinal adjectives:** These refer to cardinal numbers such as one, three, eight.

# Adjectives

**Ordinal adjectives:** These refer to ordinal numbers that describe the exact place of a noun in a group. For example: fourth, ninth

**Fraction adjectives:** These refer to a number that is less than one.
For example: one-third, a quarter

Numeral adjectives are also called **determiners** since they determine the kind of reference a noun/noun group has.
For example: every, the, a

Did you notice that **the** and **a** are articles but they become quantitative adjectives too?
For example: a cat, the cat

Some adjectives show emphasis and are called **emphasising adjectives.**
For example: This is a total waste of money.
He is standing at the very end of the platform.
**Total** and **very** emphasise (describe) the nouns **waste** and **end.**

Remember that an adjective is not always in front of the noun.
For example: It is easy to complete the work in time.

## Interrogative adjectives and interrogative pronouns

Interrogative adjectives are those that ask questions.
For example: Which boy has gone out of the class?
What presents did you give her?
**Which** and **What** are referring to the noun **class** and pronoun **her.**

Interrogative pronouns also ask questions. Notice the difference.

| Interrogative Adjectives | Interrogative Pronouns |
|---|---|
| Which classes did you take? | Which did you like? |
| Whose phone did you use? | Whose did you break? |
| What kind of pronoun is it? | What is a pronoun? |

*whose, which, what*
As interrogative pronouns: Which did you prefer? Whose is it?
As interrogative adjectives: [Which quiz] did you take? [Whose car] did you see?

# Adjectives

## Possessive pronouns and possessive adjectives

Notice the use of **his**.

For example: Is this his? (pronoun)

He has lost his book. (adjective)

Remember adjectives depend on nouns.

For example: He has lost his book.

We cannot say: He has lost his ______.

**His** (possessive adjective) comes before the noun **book**.

A possessive adjective comes before a noun and a possessive pronoun comes after a noun.

## Similes

Adjectives are used in similes — a figure of speech which compares one thing to another to provide a clearer word picture of something or someone.

For example: as light as a feather, as white as snow

## Antonyms

Adjectives describe nouns. Adjectives also show opposite ways of describing nouns. Antonyms are adjectives with opposite meanings.

For example, dull/bright day, sweet/sour oranges, rough/smooth road, fresh/stale cake, short/tall man

# Adjectives

- **Grammar Game**

Divide the class into four groups—A, B, C and D.

Start with Group A. The first student in Group A starts with one word—a noun.

For example: princess

The second student in Group A adds another word to the noun (preferably an adjective).

For example: beautiful princess

The third child adds an article or adjective.

For example: The beautiful princess.....

The fourth child adds a verb, a conjunction or a preposition.

For example: The beautiful princess was awakened.....

This activity can continue till all the members of one group get a chance to add new words.

This exercise can be repeated with the other groups.

This game is a good way to revise all the parts of speech.

# Adjectives

**Types of adjectives: quantitative adjectives**
**interrogative adjectives**
**possessive adjectives**

## 1 Read the following sentences and identify the types of adjectives.

*a* Which car do you drive? __________

*b* Only one boy is absent, all the rest are present. __________ __________ ________

*c* After eating the cake, he drank some water. __________

*d* All the glasses are washed. Every glass is clean. __________ __________

*e* There is too much pollution in this area. ________

*f* They will go to her house. ________

*g* Several people were injured in a bus accident. ________

*h* This is the fifth time I have got fifty marks. ________ ________

*i* From the very beginning he has been a diligent boy.

*j* These shoes are mine. ___________

## 2 Rewrite the following sentences using antonyms of the underlined words.

*a* Ram always remembers to bring his books to school.

______________________________________________

*b* They were happy to hear of his arrival.

______________________________________________

*c* They went through the entrance, which was narrow and dark.

______________________________________________

*d* He approved of my work.

______________________________________________

*e* The majority of the people in this village are old.

______________________________________________

*f* She spoke politely.

______________________________________________

*g* Badminton is generally played outdoors.

______________________________________________

*h* It is easier to multiply than to subtract.

______________________________________________

*i* He accepted what I said.

______________________________________________

# Adjectives of Degree

**Adjectives of degree show how people and things compare with each other. There are three degrees: positive, comparative and superlative.**

When an adjective already ends in a suffix, we add ***more*** and ***most*** to show comparative and superlative degrees.

## 1 Highlight the correct word–**more** or **most**.

*a* That is the (more most) beautiful sunset I have ever seen!

*b* The main bedroom is (more most) spacious than all the others.

*c* Tony is the (more most) adventurous person in our group.

*d* The machine will be (more most) efficient if you oil the motor.

*e* Tina's picture is (more most) colourful than mine.

## 2 Add **more** or **most** to the following sentences.

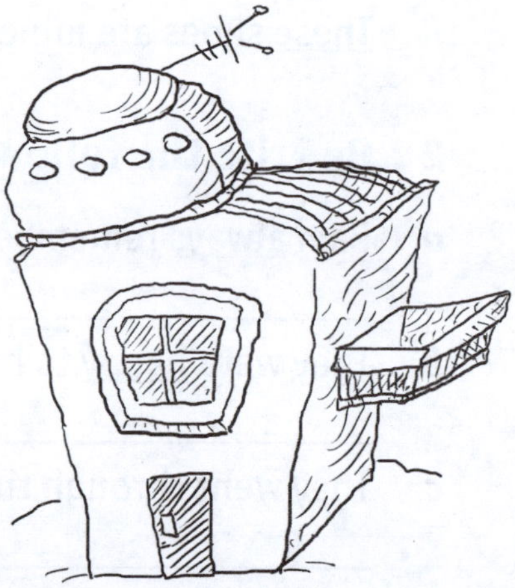

*a* That is the ___________ unusual building I have ever seen.

*b* Kaushik grew ___________ despondent as each day passed.

*c* The director told us she needed a ___________ dramatic performance.

*d* Is the taipan the ___________ venomous snake found in Australia?

*e* Sitting in the dentist's waiting room, I became ___________ and ___________ nervous.

## 3 Complete the sentences by using the correct degree.

*a* He is the ______________________ composer I know. (famous)

*b* Ajay is ______________________ than his older brother now. (big)

*c* Ask Shelley, she is ______________________ than John. (reliable)

*d* March, this year, was the ______________________ on record. (dry)

*e* She became ______________________ when her friends came to visit. (cheerful)

# Adjectives in Context

**Adjectives play an important role in describing the characters in a story and the backdrop against which they perform.**

## 1 Highlight at least ten adjectives in this description.

I was not prepared for Professor Splott. He oozed into the room like a long, brown stick insect. He was taller than I thought anyone could be, and his long face was like stretched chewing gum. His bald head shone like a polished egg. He stalked across the room, his long, skinny, bony fingers clutching a short stick. His beady brown eyes bored into my brain. "Well, Brown, what have you done this time?" he said in a menacing kind of way.

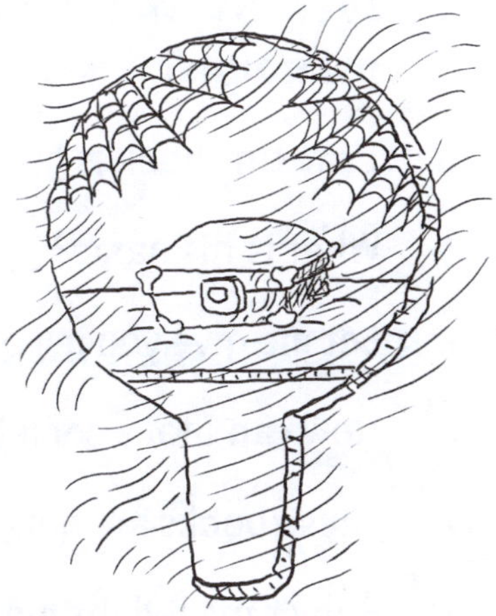

## 2 Fill in the missing adjectives using words from the box below.

An ____________ sandstone house rose out of the ____________ wood.

In the distance, thunder crackled, and ____________ flashes of lightning lit up the ____________ roof and ____________ shutters. The two children moved cautiously toward the heavy ____________ door. It looked solid and impassive. Priya peered through the large keyhole. Flashes of lightning lit up a single box in the centre of an ____________ room. It was a large, ____________, wooden box with a curved lid and ____________ brass latches. Her eyes took in the long, ____________ cobwebs in the high corners of the room and the deep scratches on the walls. A dank, ____________ smell filled her nostrils.

She felt strangely excited...

| | | | | | |
|---|---|---|---|---|---|
| broken | empty | carved | dark | wooden | strange |
| brief | shiny | old | decaying | draping | falling |

## 3 On a piece of paper, draw the three characters in this interaction. Construct a web of adjectives around each one to give them life and personality.

"Sit, Toby, sit!" commanded Amit, smacking the dog hard across the nose with a thin stick. Toby lowered his head and whimpered.

"Stop that, Amit!" shouted Shalini, throwing her arms around Toby's neck.

# Possessive Adjectives and Pronouns

**A possessive adjective comes before a noun and a possessive pronoun comes after a noun.**

**1 Identify whether the underlined words are possessive adjectives or possessive pronouns.**

*a* I say this book is hers. She says it is mine. ________ ________

*b* What is his name? __________

*c* Let me give you my pencil. _________

*d* How can I take something that is yours? ________

*e* These books are hers. ______

*f* Baby finished his meal. ________

*g* These toys are theirs, not mine. _________ _________

*h* Are you home? I am. _________ _________

**2 Fill in the blanks with appropriate possessive adjectives or pronouns.**

*a* Have _______ visited the new mall?

*b* ______ shall put on _______ shirt as ______ has gone for washing.

*c* The travellers lost all ________baggage while changing trains.

*d* Roma said, "Thank ______."

*e* Has anyone seen ______?

*f* _______ are going to play in the park. Would _______ like to join us?

*g* _______ shirt had a hole in ______.

WORK SHEET 15

# Adjectives in Similes

**Adjectives are often used in similes. Similes paint a clear picture by showing how one thing is like something else. For example:** as cold as ice; as old as the hills; as flat as a pancake.

**1 Circle the simile in each sentence.**

*a* Dad told me to be as quiet as a mouse.

*b* She was as busy as a bee in the garden.

*c* The road was as straight as an arrow.

*d* Last night the sky was as black as ink.

*e* Her face was as pale as a ghost.

**2 Complete these similes using words from the box.**

*a* As gentle as a ________________

*b* As light as a ________________

*c* As sick as a ________________

*d* As clear as a ________________

*e* As white as ________________

*f* As cool as a ________________

*g* As blind as a ________________

| *snow* |
|---|
| *crystal* |
| *bat* |
| *cucumber* |
| *feather* |
| *dog* |
| *lamb* |

**3 Write some similes of your own.**

*a* Her eyes are as brown as ____________________.

*b* This chair is as hard as ____________________.

*c* The villagers were as poor as ____________________.

*d* My shoes are as shiny as ____________________.

*e* The river is as wide as ____________________.

*f* She felt as young as a ____________________.

*g* The moon is as silent as ____________________.

*h* That was as funny as ____________________.

**4 Choose any simile and use it in a sentence.**

________________________________________

WORK SHEET 16

# Adjectives in Similes

**Adjectives are often used in similes. Similes paint a clear picture by saying how one thing is like something else. For example:** as cold as ice; as old as the hills; as white as snow.

## 1 Spot the simile in each sentence and circle it.

*a* During the performance, you must be as quiet as a mouse.

*b* I can't understand this question. It's as clear as mud.

*c* My father taught me many things. He is as wise as an owl.

*d* Be careful of the broken glass. It's as sharp as a knife.

*e* The water is frozen. It's as hard as a rock.

## 2 Complete these similes using words from the box.

*a* as cunning as a ____________

*b* as smooth as ____________

*c* as high as the ____________

*d* as pretty as a ____________

*e* as wise as an ____________

*f* as cold as ____________

*g* as regular as ____________

*h* as deep as the ____________

| |
|---|
| *silk* |
| *picture* |
| *clockwork* |
| *owl* |
| *ice* |
| *ocean* |
| *sky* |
| *fox* |

## 3 Write some similes of your own.

as blue as ____________

as hard as ____________

as poor as ____________

as shiny as ____________

as silent as ____________

as pleased as ____________

as young as ____________

as wide as ____________

as old as ____________

as clever as ____________

as green as ____________

as sad as ____________

## 4 Choose any three similes and use them in sentences.

______________________________________________

______________________________________________

______________________________________________

# Verbs

Verbs consist of one or more words that show the particular interactions and relationships between people, places, events and objects.

Helping verbs are also called **auxiliary verbs**. They are used with present and past participles to make a complete verb. Their job is to show tense and possibility.

For example: We are eating dinner. They were eating chips.

## Subject-Verb Agreement

A sentence contains a subject and a predicate. The subject has no verb; the predicate contains the verb. We can know about the subject by asking the question who or what in addition to the predicate.

Look at the sentence: The rat ran into the kitchen.

In this sentence we ask the question 'who ran into the kitchen?' to get the subject.

The subject can be made up of noun/nouns/a word or group of words, which perform the work of a noun.

The subject very often includes an article, an adjective or a conjunction.

The subject word(s) are also called the simple subject.

Since the nouns are singular or plural, a subject in the sentence is singular or plural. Remember that the verb must agree with the subject in number and in person.

If a subject is singular, the verb must be singular and if the subject is plural, so must be the verb.

The form of the verb will depend on the person of the subject. Remember that for all verbs, all nouns should be considered as pronouns of the third person.

Read the following sentences.

1. I am cooking.
2. We are cooking.
3. They/You enjoy sports
4. He/She enjoys sports.
5. A dog barks.
6. Dogs bark.

1. I (noun/pronoun) is singular (first person), hence the verb am cooking is singular (first person).
2. We is plural (first person), hence the verb are cooking is plural (first person).
3. They/You is plural (third/second), hence the verb enjoy is singular.
4. She/He/Dog is singular (third person), hence the verb enjoys/barks is singular.
5. Dogs is plural (third person), hence the verb bark is singular (third person).

# Verbs

The pronoun I is a little special.

Read the following sentences.

1 I am a girl.
2 I am going.
3 I was going.
4 I go.
5 I have gone.

I is singular and takes a singular verb—am, am going, was going.

But in sentences 4 and 5 it takes a plural form because in present and present perfect tenses, it takes a plural form.

## I and the future perfect tense

I shall have gone.

He will have gone.

In both these cases I is singular whereas **shall have** and **will have** are plural form of the word.

## Transitive and Intransitive Verbs

Verbs that require an object after it to complete the sense are called transitive verbs.

For example: The dog bit the farmer.

The farmer is the object and without the object, the sentence doesn't make sense. Just saying **The dog bit** is incomplete.

An intransitive verb does not require an object to make sense. It makes perfect sense on its own, without the object.

For example: The fire burns.
Birds fly.

The **present participle** is formed by adding –ing to the infinitive.

For example: fly, flying; jump, jumping

The **past participle** is formed by adding –ed to the infinitive.

For example: kick, kicked; play, played

The past participle can also be used as an adjective.

For example: baked food.

The past participle is also used to form other tenses such as the present tenses.

For example: He has gone to Delhi. (perfect present)
The children had worked hard. (perfect past)
You will have completed the task by then. (perfect future)

# Verbs

**A verb group is a group of words built around a verb. They contain helping verbs, participles or infinitives. For example:** Tahir wanted to go early. Verb groups indicate the processes in text.

***Meet the Helpers!***
*am, is, are, was, were, be, being, been, do, does, did, has, have, had, shall, will, can, must, may, might, could, would, should*

*a* Our family is flying to Canada in May.
*b* You could come with us to the tennis game.
*c* Jane has been waiting for her plane for three hours.
*d* We might go to the movies this afternoon.
*e* They are having a good time at the party.

*a* I will be ________________ in the cricket match on Saturday.
*b* He has been ________________ in the school pool.
*c* Next week I will be ________________ my birthday.
*d* I can ________________ as well as you can.
*e* After their long trek, they were ________________.

Some helpers show:
- **Possibility**: *I **may** go. He **might** come.*
- **Ability**: *Bees **can** produce honey. They **could** ride their bikes.*
- **Obligation**: *You **must** stay indoors. She **should** save her money.*

The choice of helping verb can subtly change a message.

*a* The problem of global warming ________ be solved. (show obligation)
*b* Scientists ______ discover life on other planets. (show possibility)
*c* Recycled water _______ solve the problem of water shortages. (show ability)
*d* All assignments ________ be handed in by next Friday. (show obligation)
*e* If it rains, the game _______ end in a draw. (show possibility)

WORK SHEET 18

# Verbs

**A sentence can be made negative by placing not or never after the helper, for example:** I have not eaten yet. They will never win the game. She cannot see without glasses.

**1 Underline the verb groups.**

The first one has been done for you

*a* Autumn leaves have just started to fall.

*b* Meghna has always been my friend.

*c* The voters will probably elect a new president.

*d* Did you know that a new planet has recently been discovered?

*e* He will be sadly missed by us all.

*f* You can always depend on Lalit to help.

**2 Rewrite the sentences in their negative form.**

*a* I can take you with me.

______________________________

*b* You might see him tomorrow.

______________________________

*c* We will be travelling to the coast in June.

______________________________

*d* The surfers should wait for the tide to turn.

______________________________

*e* The bushfire is burning across the eastern ridge.

______________________________

**3 Complete these negative statements.**

*a* They could not see ______________________________

*b* Bano did not like ______________________________

*c* I have never seen ______________________________

*d* Maggie does not want ______________________________

*e* The teacher might not let us ______________________________

# Verbs in Narrative

**Verbs play a colourful role in story writing. Writers recognise the power in verbs to create strong images of movement, action and behaviour. Most narratives are written in the past tense. Dialogue, however, can slip from one tense to another.**

## 1 Highlight at least twenty past tense verbs in this story extract.

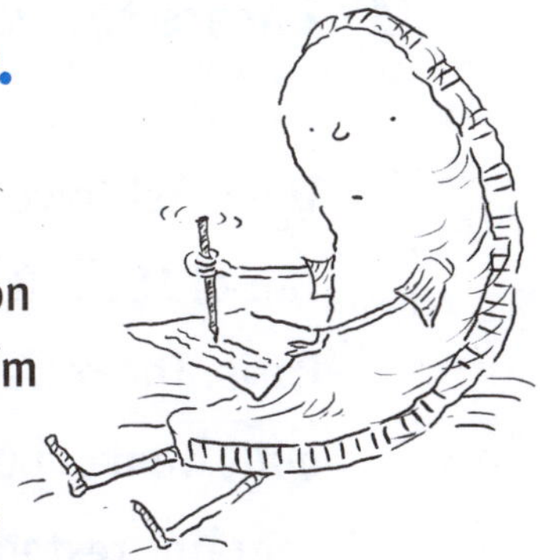

### *The Tale of a Fifty-paise Coin*

I clearly remember that Thursday—the Thursday that changed my life forever. It started quietly enough. I lay with an odd assortment of coins on Mr Malik's bedside table. He usually left me behind these days—I guess I'm just not worth much anymore.

Not so today. Today was different. I felt myself being scooped up with the rest of the coins and dropped with a jingle, deep into a trouser pocket. Squashed at the bottom, I was uncomfortable and more than a little breathless.

As Mr Malik waited for the bus, he wrapped his podgy fingers around a bunch of coins, with me in the middle. He took us out of his pocket and spread us out on his palm. I guessed he was counting out his fare. I couldn't help but think that I wouldn't be of any use to him, not with all those smart one and two rupee coins.

Just then the bus appeared at the corner. Mr Malik closed his hand, but I felt myself slipping through the crack in his fingers. The thunder of the approaching bus swallowed my cries as I fell and hit the footpath spinning and jarring. The crunch of a boot grazed my side and sent me flinging end over end into the street. The world spun out of control as I rolled helplessly towards a grate. Then I was falling noiselessly, down, down, down.

I landed in a soft puff of dust. Then all was silent. So silent. At the bottom of my prison all was dark and dank and cold and dusty.

## 2 Now continue the story with some verbs of your own choice.

I don't know how long I ____________ there in the silence. I lost track of time.

I __________ that I was back in Mr Malik's room. I thought about all the rooms I'd been in, all the pockets and purses, and all the hands I'd passed between.

Suddenly, something ______________ my reverie. I listened. Rain? Unmistakably rain. I could __________ it far above. I could ____________ its wet fingers as it gathered and ______________ into my prison, turning my bed into mud, then lifting me and carrying me along in its strengthening flow. Faster and faster I was ___________dizzily through a web of interconnecting tunnels. I was _____________ in the torrent now, but glad to be free of the silent dust...

WORK SHEET 20

# Verbs in Reports

**Verbs play an important part in passing on factual information. They are definite about the way things are.**
**For example:** Mt Everest is the tallest mountain ...
Parrots live on a diet of fruit, seeds ...

**1 Locate the verbs in this report. Make an observation about tense.**

***The Eiffel Tower***

The Eiffel Tower was designed by Gustave Eiffel for the World's Fair of 1889. It stands 352 metres above the Champs de Mars in Paris. The tower is an elegant wrought-iron skeleton structure built from 6400 metric tons of iron and steel. The Eiffel Tower contains restaurants, and a television and weather station. Lifts and stairs lead to the top. For many years the Eiffel Tower was the highest structure in the world.

Observation: ________________________________________

________________________________________

**2 Add the missing verbs to this report on mosquitoes.**

Mosquitoes ______ very small, slender, frail insects. They ______ only two wings and ________ found in all parts of India.

Mosquitoes breed in still water during the warmer months of the year. The female mosquito ______ blood from humans so she is able to ______ her eggs.

Mosquito bites ______ swollen itchy spots on the skin that ______ very irritating. In many parts of the world, mosquitoes ________ diseases such as yellow fever and malaria. Many humans have died as a result of mosquito bites.

In India, most mosquitoes are harmless though annoying. Some, however, ______ carriers of diseases such as dengue fever and malaria. Although they ______ small and fragile, mosquitoes remain the most irritating of all insects to humans.

# Subject-Verb Agreement

**The form of the verb will depend on the person of the subject. A verb must agree with the subject in number and in person.**

## 1 Fill in the blanks with correct verb forms.

*a* You ________ (has have) done your work very well.

*b* When he ________ (goes go) to the market he will buy toys.

*c* You must _______ (tell tells) your sister that she must not _____ (does do) anything to upset me.

*d* My parents always _______ (guide guides) me to _______ (speak speaks) gently.

*e* Ashu's pet dog _______ (barks bark) at everyone who _______(visit visits) them. I was lucky that he did not even _______ (whimpers whimper) at me.

*f* I ______ (enjoys enjoy) a glass of milk every night. My father also ______ (loves love) to ______ (have has) it.

## 2 Match the group of words in Column A with Column B to form meaningful sentences.

| | Column A | Column B |
|---|---|---|
| *a* | He and his father | finished her work. |
| *b* | Susan has not | start in a few minutes. |
| *c* | Sonia has decided | going to open on Wednesday. |
| *d* | The show will | to visit Raman. |
| *e* | Our school is | were sleeping. |

*a* ____________________________________________

*b* ____________________________________________

*c* ____________________________________________

*d* ____________________________________________

*e* ____________________________________________

# Subject-Verb Agreement

**A verb gives a sentence a reason for 'being'. It informs of some process occurring between people and things. In the fast growing world of telecommunications we have new verbs such as email, text, autoformat etc.**

## 1 Correct the following sentences.

*a* Did you taken my book?

______________________________

*b* There are dark cloud in the sky.

______________________________

*c* She were playing while they was cleaning the room.

______________________________

*d* I is going to the market and will bought a frock.

______________________________

*e* Peter are in bed and Mohan are troubling him.

______________________________

*f* When is they coming back from where he have gone?

______________________________

## 2 Underline the verbs.

*a* I will have given my dresses for washing.

*b* He had lost the way and reached home late.

*c* The carpenters have completed the task.

*d* Who has taken James' pen?

*e* They will have eaten their lunch by 2 p.m.

*f* Who has told you about me?

*g* I have walked two kilometres.

WORK SHEET 23

# Transitive -Intransitive Verbs

**When a verb has an object that receives the action of the verb, we say that the verb is transitive. For example:** I sold some dresses. I wrote an essay.
**A verb is intransitive when it doesn't have an object after it. For example:** He slept. Priya coughed.

**1 Fill in the blanks with the –ing form of the verb.**

*a* A cow is __________ in the river.

*b* The farmer is ___________ a tractor.

*c* She was _________ the packet with a string.

*d* She was _________ in the cold.

*e* The clock is _______.

*f* The gardener is _______ a hole in the ground.

*g* She was ________ her nails.

*h* Pieces of paper were _______ on the floor.

**2 Read the following sentences. Identify the transitive (TR) and intransitive (ITR) verbs and the object to complete the table given on the next page.**

The first two are done for you in the table.

*a* The crows are cawing.

*b* The boys ate cakes.

*c* The girls sang songs.

*d* The rain started.

*e* The children are smelling flowers.

*f* The servant cooked the dinner.

*g* The clouds were floating.

*h* The farmer grows wheat.

*i* Mummy is cleaning the closet.

*j* The grocer sells tea.

*k* He fought well.

*l* Who rang the bell?

WORK SHEET 23

# Transitive -Intransitive Verbs

**A transitive verb is linked to a noun object, whereas an intransitive verb does not have an object after it.**

| Transitive | Object | Intransitive |
|---|---|---|
| | | are cawing |
| ate | cakes | |
| | | |
| | | |
| | | |
| | | |
| | | |
| | | |
| | | |
| | | |
| | | |
| | | |

**WORK SHEET 24**

# Verbs - Contractions

**Many negative verbs are written as contractions. For example:**
did not = didn't  is not = isn't  have not = haven't.

The helping verb and *not* contract into one word. An apostrophe replaces the 'o' in *not*.

*a* We <u>couldn't</u> enter the store until 9:00 am. ( **could not** )

*b* The disappointed crowd didn't wait for the final score. (  )

*c* Shouldn't you be in bed? (  )

*d* Kavita hasn't seen a lunar eclipse before. (  )

*e* It isn't raining yet. (  )

*f* Gautam wasn't driving a red Ferrari. (  )

| *a* doesn't | had not |
|---|---|
| *b* won't | were not |
| *c* hadn't | does not |
| *d* weren't | will not |

| *e* didn't | would not |
|---|---|
| *f* wouldn't | was not |
| *g* can't | cannot |
| *h* wasn't | did not |

| *i* haven't | do not |
|---|---|
| *j* aren't | have not |
| *k* don't | could not |
| *l* couldn't | are not |

*a* The men are diving for pearls. ______________________

*b* He was climbing up onto the roof. ______________________

*c* Do you have a home computer? ______________________

*d* The table has been set for dinner. ______________________

*a* His friends aren't ______________________.

*b* Won't you come ______________________?

*c* She hasn't bought ______________________.

# Verbs - Contractions

**Many subjects and verbs are written as contractions, for example:** she will = she'll  I would = I'd  we have = we've  they are = they're

**Usually, a pronoun subject and a helping verb contract to one word. An apostrophe marks the missing letters. For example: *You've*** been eating strawberries!

**1 Match and colour the contractions with the words they replace. Use a different colour for each contraction.**

| I'll | they have |
|---|---|
| he's | you have |
| they've | I will |
| we're | she would |
| she'd | he is |
| you've | we are |

| I'm | it is |
|---|---|
| you're | we have |
| they're | you are |
| it's | he will |
| he'll | they are |
| we've | I am |

| I've | we will |
|---|---|
| you'll | they would |
| he'd | you will |
| she's | I have |
| they'd | he would |
| we'll | she is |

**2 Circle the contractions. Write the two words in full.**

*a* She knew (I'd) seen the movie before. ( I had )

*b* I'm so glad that you're finally here. (__________) (__________)

*c* We'd like her to come home when she's finished. (__________) (__________)

*d* It's exciting to think that we'll soon be in Prague. (__________) (__________)

*e* You'll be surprised how tall he's grown. (__________) (__________)

*f* They're late. I wonder if they've lost their way. (__________) (__________)

**3 Highlight the correct word in the brackets.**

*a* If (your you're) sure (its it's) safe, I'll come with you.

*b* (There They're) very far from their seaside home.

*c* (Where We're) leaving on the five o'clock train.

*d* Didn't you know that we (were we're) leaving?

*e* (Were We're) sure (its it's) the best thing to do.

# Verb Tense

The tense of a verb tells us the time of an action. The time can be — past, present or future.

I play.(present tense)
I played. (past tense)
I will play. (future tense)

Each tense can be expressed in four different ways. These are four forms of the present tense:
**Simple present tense:** This tense is used to show fact or truth and for actions done regularly. It does not tell us whether the action is complete or incomplete.
For example: I play. I work. Rohan goes to school everyday.
**Present continuous tense:** This tense expresses an action that is still going on or in continuation. It tells us that the action is still incomplete.
For example: I am eating. He is swimming.
**Present perfect tense:** This tense tells us that the action is completed or 'perfected'.
For example: I have worked. He has eaten.
**Present perfect continuous tense:** This tense shows that the action has been going on continuously up to the present time.
For example: He has been swimming. I have been eating.

The past and the future tense also have four forms.

### Past tense

Simple past: I ate.
Past continuous: I was eating.
Past perfect: I had eaten.
Past perfect continuous: I had been eating.

### Future tense

Simple future: I will/shall eat.
Future continuous: I will/shall be eating.
Future perfect: I will/shall have eaten.
Future perfect continuous: I will/shall have been eating.

# Verb Tense

***when***

| in the **present** | in the **past** | in the **future** |
|---|---|---|
| The plane *is flying*. | The plane *flew*. | The plane *will fly*. |

***present***

- the infinitive — singular – He **plays** football. / plural – They **play** football.
- the (present) participle with a helper — singular – He football. / plural – They football.

***past***

- the (past) participle — singular – He **played** football. / plural – They **played** football.
- the (present) participle with a helper — singular – He **was playing** football. – He **has been playing** football. / plural – They **were playing** football. – They **have been playing** football.
- the (past) participle with a helper — singular – He **has played** football. / plural – They **have played** football.

***future***

- the infinitive with the helpers *shall* and *will* — singular – He **will play** football. / plural – They **will play** football.
- *may* and *might* indicate a possible future — singular – He football. / plural – They football.
- Future tense can be shown in other ways: I football.

, I football. I

football.

# Verb Tense

**Tenses allow speakers and writers to express exactly what they want to say.**

| Tense | Number | 1st person | 2nd person | 3rd person |
|---|---|---|---|---|
| *Simple present* | Singular | I fish | You **eat** fish. | He/she/it **eats** fish. |
| | Plural | We fish. | You **eat** fish. | They **eat** fish. |
| *Present continuous* | Singular | I fish. | You **are eating** fish. | He/she/it **is eating** fish. |
| | Plural | We fish. | You **are eating** fish. | They **are eating** fish. |
| *Present perfect* | Singular | I fish. | You **have eaten** fish. | He/she/it **has eaten** fish. |
| | Plural | We fish. | You **have eaten** fish. | They **have eaten** fish. |
| *Perfect continuous* | Singular | I fish. | You **have been eating** fish. | He/she/it **has been eating** fish. |
| | Plural | We fish. | You **have been eating** fish. | They **have been eating** fish. |

## PAST TENSE VERBS

| Tense | Number | 1st person | 2nd person | 3rd person |
|---|---|---|---|---|
| *Simple past* | Singular | I **ate** fish | You **ate** fish. | He/she/it **ate** fish. |
| | Plural | We **ate** fish. | You **ate** fish. | They **ate** fish. |
| *Past continuous* | Singular | I **was eating** fish. | You **were eating** fish. | He/she/it **was eating** fish. |
| | Plural | We **were eating** fish. | You **were eating** fish. | They **were eating** fish. |
| *Past perfect* | Singular | I **had eaten** fish. | You **had eaten** fish. | He/she/it **had eaten** fish. |
| | Plural | We **had eaten** fish. | You **had eaten** fish. | They **had eaten** fish. |
| *Perfect continuous* | Singular | I **had been eating** fish. | You **had been eating** fish. | He/she/it **had been eating** fish. |
| | Plural | We **had been eating** fish. | You **had been eating** fish. | They **had been eating** fish. |

## FUTURE TENSE VERBS

| Tense | Number | 1st person | 2nd person | 3rd person |
|---|---|---|---|---|
| *Simple future* | Singular | I **will eat** fish | You **will eat** fish. | He/she/it **will eat** fish. |
| | Plural | We **will eat** fish. | You **will eat** fish. | They **will eat** fish. |
| *Future continuous* | Singular | I **will be eating** fish. | You **will be eating** fish. | He/she/it **will be eating** fish. |
| | Plural | We **will be eating** fish. | You **will be eating** fish. | They **will be eating** fish. |
| *Future perfect* | Singular | I **will have eaten** fish. | You **will have eaten** fish. | He/she/it **will have eaten** fish. |
| | Plural | We **will have eaten** fish. | You **will have eaten** fish. | They **will have eaten** fish. |
| *Future perfect continuous* | Singular | I **will have been eating** fish. | You **will have been eating** fish. | He/she/it **will have been eating** fish. |
| | Plural | We **will have been eating** fish. | You **will have been eating** fish. | They **will have been eating** fish. |

We can even add other verbs to clarify our meaning. For example:

*I **could** have been eating fish. They **should** be eating fish. He **might** have eaten fish. We **can** eat fish.*

WORK SHEET 26

# Verb Tense

**Verbs tell us when things are happening. Present is happening now. Past has happened. Future is going to happen.**

**1 Identify whether the following sentences are in the past, present or future tense.**

*a* My father drives his car to work. ________

*b* John walked home from school when he missed the bus. ________

*c* I will learn to swim next season.________

*d* Ram went on a trip last year. ________

*e* They will buy me a bicycle for my birthday next month. ________

*f* She will wish the teacher tomorrow morning. ________

**2 Rewrite each sentence using a verb in the past tense.**

*a* The storm interrupts the electricity.

________________________________________

*b* He is wearing a lovely watch.

________________________________________

*c* Residents stream into the shelters.

________________________________________

*d* A skateboard takes you everywhere.

________________________________________

WORK SHEET 27

# Verb Tense

**The continuous tenses are used when talking about a particular point in time. For example:** I am shopping at the mall. He is washing his car.

**1 Fill in the continuous form of the verbs and make sentences.**

| Verb | -ing | Sentence |
|---|---|---|
| sing | | |
| go | | |
| lie | | |

**2 Make a ladder of verbs beginning with 'T'. The ladder begins with three letters and goes up to 10 letters. You may use any form of the verb.**

| | | | | | | | | | |
|---|---|---|---|---|---|---|---|---|---|
| | | | | | | | T | | |
| | | | | | | T | | | |
| | | | | | T | | | | |
| | | | | T | | | | | |
| | | | T | | | | | | |
| | | T | | | | | | | |
| | T | | | | | | | | |
| T | | | | | | | | | |

# Verb Tense

**3 Fill in the blanks with verbs in brackets as per the tense mentioned at the end of the sentence.**

*a* After she ____________ (hear) the good news, she ____________ (begin) to ring up her friend. [Past perfect]

*b* I have some good news for you. You ____________ (stand) first in the test. [Present perfect]

*c* He hasn't a rupee with him. He ____________ (spend) all his money. [Present perfect]

*d* By the end of the month they ____________ (arrive) in India. [Future perfect]

*e* They stopped working after the sun ____________ (set). [Past perfect]

*f* He ____________ (call) you in the next hour. [Future perfect]

**4 Solve the following crossword puzzle with the help of the clues.**

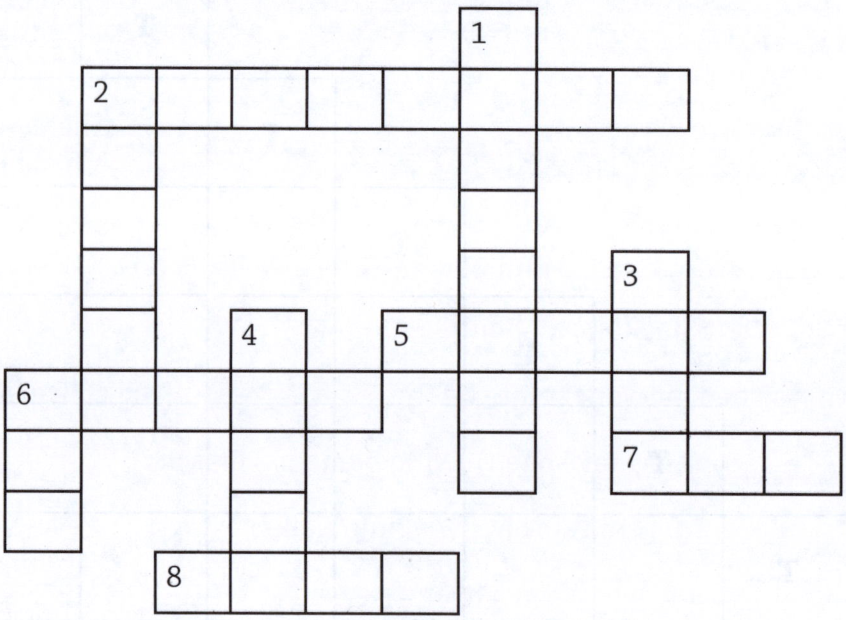


**Across**

2 the ball is ____________

5 when we go to someone's house, it is to do this

6 to begin

7 we use our mouth to do this

8 I went to her house to ________ her

**Down**

1 the girls were ________

2 she ________ a pair of shoes

3 please ________ me your ball

4 we do this with a pencil

6 we do this with our eyes

WORK SHEET 29

# Verb Tense

**Each tense can be expressed as—simple tense, continuous tense, perfect tense, perfect continous tense.**

## 1 Fill in the blanks with the correct word from the brackets.

*a* Roma __________ clothes every day. (is washing/washes)

*b* My brother ______________ his homework now. (was doing/is doing)

*c* She is always ______________ of a headache. (complaining/complains)

*d* The carnival __________ over several days ago. (was/has been)

*e* My friends _________ yesterday. (came/come)

*f* I __________ to Cochin. (will go/am going)

*g* Mr Rao ______________ unconscious since last week. (has been/was)

*h* The roof ______________ during the storm last week. (breaks/broke)

*i* Sam _____________ in Delhi for fifteen years. (has lived/had lived)

*j* How I wish my mom ________ here! (were/was)

*k* By this time tomorrow, you _________________________ home. (shall reach/shall have reached)

*l* It _________________________ raining all night. (has been/is)

*m* He __________ (left/had left) an hour ago.

*n* I shall have finished my work before he ________________. (will arrive/arrives)

*o* I ________________ (am /have been) living here for a month.

*p* My sister ______________ too slowly. (walking/walks)

*q* Mr Ahuja is ________________ a movie on television. (watches/watching)

# Revision 1

1 Complete the following table of singular and plural nouns.

| Singular | Plural |
|---|---|
| key | |
| fox | |
| puppy | |
| wolf | |
| cargo | |
| goose | |
| watch | |
| | furniture |

2 Unscramble the letters in brackets to find the gender pair of the following.

*a* lion (eslsino) ________

*b* brother (tiser) ________

*c* madam (rsi) ________

*d* hero (ineeohr) ________

*e* king (nqeue) ________

*f* duchess (edku) ________

*g* gentleman (namowteenlg) ________

*h* niece (hwnpee) ________

3 Circle the odd word. Give your reason.

| | | | | | |
|---|---|---|---|---|---|
| *a* | water | weather | sheep | music | ________ |
| *b* | anger | dust | aircraft | cream | ________ |
| *c* | key | bunch | herd | shoal | ________ |
| *d* | pen | book | eraser | cream | ________ |

# Revision 1

4 Highlight the noun phrases.

*a* Sleeping early at night is a good habit.

*b* I enjoy watching the discovery channel.

*c* My father doesn't like eating vegetables.

*d* It is not easy crossing the road.

*e* Everyone in the train was angry at the delay.

*f* No one likes working on a Sunday.

5 Complete the noun groups and make sentences with them.

Humid and wet ________

______________________________________________________________

Brave and adventurous __________

______________________________________________________________

6 Circle the verbal nouns in the sentences.

*a* Oragami is the art of paper folding.

*b* My friend does skating.

*c* Rock climbing requires special boots.

*d* Reading is an interesting activity.

7 Fill in the blanks with verbal nouns of your choice.

*a* My grandfather loves __________.

*b* We heard the roaring lions __________.

*c* ________ scared the sheep.

*d* There is not enough _________.

8 Write the pairs of abstract nouns that are similar in meaning.

*a* courage ______________

*b* love ______________

*c* cleverness ______________

*d* affection ______________

*e* intelligence ______________

*f* bravery ______________

## Revision 1

9 Use a helping verb to complete the following sentences. Remember that such verbs show **possibility**, **ability** and **obligation**.

*a* The projects ________ be completed by Tuesday.

*b* Though the children are young, they ________ ride bicycles.

*c* I ________ go to Manali next week.

*d* You ________ develop the habit of saving money.

10 Underline the verb groups.

*a* They will be lovingly remembered by all.

*b* He will be preparing for his examination.

*c* The committee will most likely elect a new secretary.

*d* Did you know that a new satellite has been sent up in space?

11 Compete the following negative sentences.

*a* I could not hear ________________________.

*b* They did not like ________________________.

*c* We do not know ________________________.

*d* The students might not ________________________.

12 Expand the following verb contractions.

He'd ______________

It's ______________

You're ______________

They'll ______________

We've ______________

I've ______________

13 Identify the transitive and intransitive verbs in the following sentences.

*a* He has always stood by me. ____________________

*b* They appeared happy. ____________________

*c* Vishnu called John a clever boy. ____________________

*d* Why blame me? ____________________

# Revision 1

14 Rewrite the following sentences in correct subject-verb agreement.

*a* The queen wear a crown.

_______________

*b* Bats flies at night.

_______________

*c* The travellers wishes to sleep in a hotel.

_______________

*d* The man were sent home.

_______________

15 Underline the verbs, rewrite the sentences using the –ing form of the word.

*a* She bit her nails.

_______________

*b* They ate spaghetti for dinner.

_______________

*c* We shiver on seeing a lion.

_______________

*d* Farmers ride a tractor.

_______________

16 Fill in the blanks with the verbs in brackets according to the tense mentioned at the end of the sentence.

*a* I have some good news for you. Your father _______________ (get) a promotion. [Present perfect]

*b* I _______________ (ring) her up tomorrow. [Future perfect]

*c* They stopped working after they _______________ (reach) home. [Past perfect]

*d* Ram _______________ (eat) a special meal on Id. [Future perfect]

17 Write similes of your own.

*a* My shirt is as _______________.

*b* The table is as _______________.

*c* She dances as _______________.

*d* The road is _______________.

# Revision 1

18 Fill in the blanks with quantitative adjectives.

*a* Put __________ salt in the soup.

*b* The __________ day has been wasted waiting for the electrician.

*c* A __________ drops of oil fell on the floor.

*d* The flight was delayed due to the _______ fog.

19 Use suitable possessive adjectives to fill in the blanks.

*a* __________ letters were misplaced in the post office.

*b* Animals use _______ tails to keep away the flies.

*c* They wanted _______ house to look the neatest.

*d* The tree shed _______ leaves every autumn.

20 Complete the adjectives of degree.

| | | |
|---|---|---|
| ***a*** | Ganga is a ______________ runner than Jenny. | (fast) |
| ***b*** | Death Valley is one of the ______________ places on Earth. | (hot) |
| ***c*** | I am good at chess, but Jeff is much ______________. | (good) |
| ***d*** | Hugh is much ____________________________ than I am. | (curious) |
| ***e*** | Akshay is the ____________________________ boy I know. | (sensible) |

# Articles

Three articles—**a**, **an**, **the**—are used to signal nouns or noun groups.

| a | an | the |
|---|---|---|

- **A** and **an** are only used with **singular** nouns. They are **indefinite** because they point to something that is not known by the reader or the listener.
- **A** is used before a word beginning with a **consonant**, for example: a rose, a computer, a clever girl.
- **An** is used before a word beginning with a **vowel**, for example: an orange, an odd person, an igloo.
- **An** is also used before a word beginning with an **'h'** (not sounded), for example: an hour, an honest man.
- **The** is a **definite** article because it points to something that has been made known to the reader or listener, for example: the cap I wear, the ball in the box.
- **The** is always used before **plural** nouns, for example: the eggs in the nest, the children at school.
- **The** is also used when it points to a common noun known by everyone, for example: the sun, the morning.

NOTE: A character in a story is usually introduced as **a**. (For example: There was once **a** giant, **a** red fox, **a** beautiful princess, **a** brave knight ...)

Once the character has been introduced, they can be referred to as **the**. (For example: **The** giant spoke ..., **The** red fox prowled ..., **The** princess lived ...)

# Articles

## Rules for using a, an and the

**A is used:**

- Before a word beginning with a consonant.
- Before vowels which have the sound **yu.**
  For example: a union, a university, a unit
- Before the word one.
  For example: a one-way street

**An is used:**

- Before words beginning with a vowel.
  For example, an egg, an umbrella
- Before a word beginning with a silent **h.**
  For example, an heir, an honest man

**The is used:**

- To refer to a particular person or thing.
  For example: the naughty boy, the big house
- With names of rivers, oceans, gulfs, mountain ranges, islands.
  For example: the Yamuna, the Andaman and Nicobar Islands
- When sacred books or newspapers are spoken of.
  For example, the Gita, the Bible, the *Indian Express*
- When we refer to directions.
  For example: the east
- When we refer to races and certain regions or nations.
  For example: the Deccan, the United States of America
- When the words kingdom, republic, state, etc. precede the name of any country.
  For example, the Republic of India
- For offices or titles.
  For example: the President of India, the King of England, the Dalai Lama

# Articles

**The is not used:**

- For names of town or cities.
- To refer to countries except the ones discussed above.
- For names of mountain peaks.
  For example: Mount Everest
- For names of historical figures.
  For example: Netaji, Akbar
- For names of streets.
  For example: Mahatama Gandhi Road, Hanuman Lane
- For the days of the week or months of the year.
- For names of precious metals, material.

WORK SHEET 30

# Articles

**'A' and 'an' are indefinite articles and 'the' is a definite article.**

**1 Fill in the blanks with the correct article.**

*a* Do you have ___ movie that I can borrow?

*b* Would you like to see ___ circus?

*c* I recommend you eat ___ chocolate pie at this restaurant.

*d* He is one of ___ smartest people I know.

*e* Can you tell me how to get to ___ school from here?

*f* This dress was designed by ___ famous New York designer.

*g* ___ children are eating their lunch.

*h* Mother Teresa was ___ Roman Catholic nun.

*i* She was ___ founder of ___ order of nuns called the Missionaries of Charity.

*j* She is wearing ___ red dress with blue shoes.

*k* Hawaii is ___ island in the Pacific Ocean.

*l* Christmas comes once ___ year.

*m* You should take ___ umbrella.

*n* Roentgen was ___ German physicist who discovered x-rays, revolutionising medical diagnosis.

*o* Albert Einstein was ___ famous scientist.

*p* Einstein left his country and lived in ___ States until he died in 1955.

*q* Put _____ clean plates away.

*r* Mum bought _____ new yellow sari.

*s* _____ winning team received _____ silver cup.

*t* He is _____ old friend of mine.

# Articles

**'The' is definite about what it names. Readers and listeners can identify what it is. For example:** the latest movie. **'A' and 'an' point to something readers and listeners only know in general terms. For example:** a fast car.

## 1 Give examples of words that will go with the following articles.

An ____________ A ____________

An ____________ A ____________

An ____________ A ____________

The ____________ The ____________

## 2 Add the correct article.

Freddo Frog was invented by Harry Melbourne for ______ McPherson Chocolates company. Freddo was going to be ______ mouse, but Harry convinced ______ company that ______ public would not like mice. Harry made _______demo Freddo and got ______ thumbs-up. ______first Freddos appeared in 1930. They were not wrapped and cost ______ penny. Now 180 million Freddo Frogs are produced annually.

# Adverbs

Adverbs are words that give more meaning to:

- a **verb** (He runs fast.)
- an **adjective** (He is a very fast runner.)
- another **adverb** (He runs too fast for me.)

Adverbs tell us how, when and where things happen.
It is easy to spot the adverb—they add meaning to verbs, adjectives and other adverbs, NEVER to nouns.

Read the following sentences.
She writes neatly.
She walked fast.
The word neatly describes how she writes and fast describes how she walks.

**Adverbs of manner**

The **ly** adverbs are adverbs that show how an action is done. They are known as **adverbs of manner**.

For example: He nodded anxiously.
She spoke slowly.

**Adverbs of time**

These adverbs tell when things happen. For example: yesterday, tomorrow, long ago, next week, on Tuesday, now

**Adverbs of time** also tell how often things happen.
For example: often, usually, once, twice, daily

**Adverbs of place**

These adverbs tell where things are happening.
For example: here, there, somewhere, around, over, away

**Adverbs of degree**

These adverbs show the extent to which something happens.
For example: very, almost, nearly, completely

# Adverbs

Adverbs, like adjectives, also have three forms:

- Positive degree: He shouted loudly.
- Comparative degree: He shouted more loudly still.
- Superlative degree: He shouted most loudly of all.

Generally, we add **–er** or **–est** to adverbs of one syllable.
For example: high, higher, highest; hard, harder, hardest
Thus, some adverbs will look like adjectives.
Remember that adverbs add meaning to verbs, adjectives and other adverbs but NEVER to nouns.

Adverbs ending in –ly are used in combination with **more** or **most** in the comparative and superlative degrees.
For example: silently, more silently, most silently
Some adverbs of degree are irregular.
For example: well, better, best; much, more, most; badly, worse, worst

## Adverbs of Frequency

Adverbs that tell us how frequently or how often something happens are known as adverbs of frequency. They are different from adverbs of time, which answer the question **When?**
Adverbs of frequency answer the question **How often?** or **How frequently?** They tell us how often somebody does something.
For example: He **never** completes his work on time.
She **always** does her work neatly.
We **sometimes** meet in the market.
Adverbs of frequency are also called mid-position adverbs. They are generally placed before a verb.
Comparative adverbs are placed before an adjective or adverb.
Some common adverbs of frequency are: always, usually, frequently, often, always, never, occasionally, rarely, seldom, hardly ever

**Interrogative adverbs** are used to ask certain questions.
For example: **How** are you? **Where** did you come from? **Why** have you come? **When** will you go?

WORK SHEET 32

# Adverbs

**Adverbs add meaning to verbs, adjectives and other adverbs. They tell us how, when and where things happen.**

**1 Fill in the blanks with suitable comparative adverbs.**

*a* Your cough is getting ________ better.

*b* He played ________ badly and lost.

*c* Try to talk ________ softly so as not to disturb the sleeping baby.

*d* He spoke ________ gently.

*e* The ________ slowly you walk, the longer you will take to reach home.

*f* My brother gets up ________ late every morning.

**Use two different comparative adverbs in the two sentences below.**

*g* Of all the people in the car, the driver was ________ / ________ seriously hurt.

*h* He walked ________ / ________ steadily although he was injured.

**2 Fill in the blanks with suitable adverbs of time.**

*a* He ________ washes his hands before eating his meals.

*b* He ________ writes to me these days.

*c* I ________ read the newspaper in the morning.

*d* I ________ talk on the phone.

*e* We ________ go to the seaside on Sunday.

*f* We ________ meet in the afternoons for coffee.

*g* There is ________ a guard at the gate.

*h* It ________ snows in a desert.

*i* Have you ________ spoken to the principal?

*j* Will you ________ listen to me?

# Adverbs

**Some adverbs of degree will look like adjectives. Remember that adverbs add meaning to verbs, adjectives and other adverbs, never to nouns.**

**1 Write two sentences for each word—first as an adverb, then as an adjective.**

Early ______________________________

______________________________

Hard ______________________________

______________________________

Round ______________________________

______________________________

**2 The adverbs are underlined. Draw a line to the verbs to which they add meaning. Do they tell how, when or where?**

*a* Niki darted <u>sideways</u> and grabbed the ball. ____________

*b* Volunteers worked <u>tirelessly</u> to repair the stadium. ____________

*c* <u>Suddenly</u>, an avalanche rolled down the mountain slope. ____________

*d* <u>There</u> she was, on a hill, painting a landscape. ____________

*e* The horse paced <u>restlessly</u> about the stable. ____________

**3 Highlight all the adverbs.**

*a* I woke very early this morning and now I'm rather tired.
*b* Nitin stood there patiently for about ten minutes.
*c* Sometimes a flock of wild geese fly noisily overhead.
*d* I screamed so loudly that the mouse scurried away quickly.
*e* My kite blew away and landed upside down in those trees.

**4 Add a suitable adverb.**

*a* He walked ____________ into the damp, dark cave. (how)

*b* ____________ I will have game of tennis with Puneet. (when)

*c* We are going __________ for a holiday in August. (where)

*d* I'll post the letter ________. (when)

WORK SHEET 34

# Adverbs - Antonyms

**Adverbs can show actions in opposite ways.**
**These adverbs are called antonyms. For example:**
Was she speaking loudly or softly?

**1 To complete each sentence, write an antonym for the adverb underlined.**

*a* The puppy ran here, ____________ and everywhere.

*b* I always come here, but he ____________ does.

*c* You go now and I'll come ____________.

*d* She did ____________ in the test, but I did badly.

*e* While Bunty went ____________, we travelled south.

**2 Write the antonyms, then complete the word search.**

strongly ____________

sadly ____________

usually ____________

forwards ____________

inside ____________

high ____________

below ____________

roughly ____________

quickly ____________

late ____________

loosely ____________

softly ____________

| | | | | | | | | | |
|---|---|---|---|---|---|---|---|---|---|
| Y | G | L | O | U | D | L | Y | K | R |
| L | S | M | O | O | T | H | L | Y | B |
| H | I | G | H | P | R | Q | K | L | D |
| G | E | A | R | L | Y | U | A | I | E |
| U | D | A | C | K | W | A | E | P | V |
| T | I | G | H | T | L | Y | W | P | O |
| R | S | D | R | A | W | K | C | A | B |
| D | T | S | L | O | W | L | Y | H | A |
| R | U | N | U | S | U | A | L | L | Y |
| L | O | W | Y | L | W | O | L | S | D |

**3 Use these words in sentences:** ***inside out upside down***

____________________________________________

____________________________________________

WORK SHEET 35

# Adverbs - Antonyms

**We can use adverbs to show actions in opposite ways. For example:** Did she speak softly or loudly? Did he do it carefully or carelessly?

Adverbs that give opposite viewpoints are called **antonyms.**

## 1 To complete each sentence, write an antonym for the adverb in brackets.

*a* That man is driving ____________________. (dangerously)

*b* The captain spoke ____________________ to his team. (loudly)

*c* He ____________________ rides his bike to school. (never)

*d* Jay treats his pet dog ____________________. (unkindly)

*e* Rita arrived ____________________ for school yesterday. (late)

*f* She will post the letter ____________________. (soon)

## 2 Search for the antonyms (opposites) of these adverbs.

smoothly
noisily
north
downwards
low
outside
loudly
above
backwards

| | | | | | | | | | |
|---|---|---|---|---|---|---|---|---|---|
| Y | L | T | F | O | S | J | O | K | R |
| L | B | G | E | L | D | W | X | L | B |
| H | I | G | H | P | R | Q | I | H | D |
| G | A | N | V | O | A | U | V | E | L |
| U | B | F | O | R | W | A | R | D | S |
| O | E | Z | E | L | P | E | F | I | O |
| R | L | G | H | Q | U | T | M | S | U |
| D | O | S | L | O | W | L | Y | N | T |
| R | W | Y | L | T | E | I | U | I | H |
| Q | U | I | E | T | L | Y | S | O | D |

## 3 Use these adverbs in sentences: *carefully* *carelessly.*

______________________________________________________________

______________________________________________________________

WORK SHEET 36

# Interrogative Adverbs

**Some adverbs are used to ask questions.**
How? When? Where? Why?
**These questions are useful when doing research and taking notes.**

<u>Where</u> is the Great Pyramid?
<u>How</u> was it constructed?
<u>When</u> was it finished?
<u>Why</u> was it built?

## 1 Complete the sentences with interrogative adverbs.

*a* ____________ did you last go fishing?
*b* ____________ are you wearing odd socks?
*c* ____________ can I buy an old rocking chair?
*d* ____________ do I get to the train station?
*e* ____________ do you leave for Thailand?

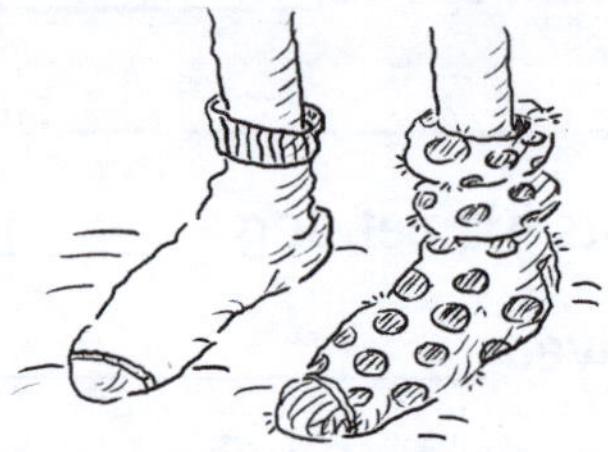

## 2 Answer the following questions.

*a* When do we celebrate Republic Day? ____________________
*b* How many legs does a horse have? ____________________
*c* Where would you buy vegetable? ____________________
*d* Why do surgeons wear gloves? ____________________
*e* Where is the Statue of Liberty? ____________________

## 3 Write five questions about this text. Ask a classmate to answer your questions.

Florence Nightingale was born in Italy in 1820, but grew up in England. The daughter of a wealthy family, she was bright and well educated. Against her parents' wishes, she decided to become a nurse. A war had broken out against Russia in the Crimean Peninsula. Florence was asked to go there to nurse the wounded soldiers. She took very great care of the men. Each night she would walk through the wards to make sure the soldiers were comfortable.

She became affectionately known as *The Lady with the Lamp*.

After the war, she returned to England in poor health and did not nurse again.

She died in 1910 at the age of ninety.

# Pronouns

Pronouns are words used in place of nouns.
For example: I , me, you, your, he, she
These are also known as **personal pronouns.** They are used to refer to ourselves, people we are talking to and people whom we are talking about. We can thus refer to three persons—one who we are talking to, the person to whom we speak and the person about whom we speak.
For example: "I told you I will not hire Ravi because he is a lazy person," Rohit told Harry.
Rohit is the speaker. The pronoun used is **I** (first-person pronoun).
Harry is the person spoken to. The pronoun used is you (second-person pronoun).
Ravi is the person spoken about. The pronoun used is he (third-person pronoun).

**Look at the table to understand personal pronouns.**

| Person | Singular | Plural |
|---|---|---|
| First | I, me, my, mine | we, us, our, ours |
| Second | you, yours | you (your), yours |
| Third | Common: it (its) | they, them, their (theirs) |
| | Masculine: he, him (his) | |
| | Feminine: she, her (hers) | |

**Possessive pronouns** show belongingness.
For example: hers, theirs
The words in brackets in the table are possessive adjectives.
For example: his chair, their books
**Interrogative pronouns** are used to ask certain questions—Who? Whom? Whose? Which? What?
For example: Who ate all the cookies?
Whom did you see?
Whose books are on the floor?
Which bus did you take?
What is your address?

**Reflexive pronouns** are those that are formed by adding -self or –selves to some of the personal pronoun forms. They can be in first, second or third person and also in singular or plural form. They can be masculine or feminine.

# Pronouns

For example: In the first person myself is singular and ourselves is plural. In the second person yourself and yourselves are in singular and plural form. In the third person, himself and herself are masculine and feminine singular forms, respectively.

Itself and themselves are common singular and all genders plural form.

In a sentence reflexive pronouns are used when the object and subject is the same person or thing.

For example: Shiela could not lift the bag herself.

Reflexive pronouns are also used for emphasising something.

For example: He himself is responsible for what has happened.

They themselves must work hard to do well.

Himself and themselves are emphasising he and they.

Sometimes we use the prepositions **by**, **to**, **with** to emphasise which person or thing we are talking about.

For example: I am angry with myself.

Shyam was eating by himself.

She is muttering to herself.

**Relative pronouns** are words that relate to a noun preceding it.

For example: I ate the cake that mother baked.

Sita is the girl who won the race.

Sometimes such pronouns act like conjunctions.

### Demonstrative pronouns

Read the following sentences.

1. This chair is strong.
2. This is the dish I enjoy eating the most.
3. These are the children who went for a picnic.
4. These students are good at their work.

In sentences 1 and 4 the demonstrative words are followed by a noun. Hence, these are demonstrative adjectives.

In sentences 2 and 3 there is no noun following the demonstrative words. Hence, they are demonstrative pronouns.

# Pronouns

**A verb is sometimes separated from its helper by another word. For example:** I have often seen him here. Did you go home early?

## 1 Highlight the pronouns in the passage.

Two roosters once had a fight to decide who would be the king of the farmyard. After a long, hard struggle one rooster could fight no more. He crept into the darkest corner of the henhouse to hide his shame. The winner flew to the top of the farmhouse, crowing and flapping his wings, to let the world know he was the new king. "Look at me!" he crowed. "I am the king of the farmyard." Just then an eagle flew by. She swooped down and seized the rooster in her talons and carried him off.

## 2 Circle ONLY the pronouns which replace Hans Christian Andersen.

Hans Christian Andersen was born in Denmark in 1805, the son of a poor shoemaker. His father died when he was only eleven years old. After attending a school for the poor, he left for Copenhagen at the age of fourteen. Here Hans met Jonas Collin who had helped him to obtain a royal scholarship, which enabled him to continue his education for the next six years. Hans was deeply unhappy and called these days "the most bitter days of my life". In 1835, he published the first of 156 fairytales. These tales made him rich and famous. He died at the age of seventy. Hans Christian Andersen is still regarded as the world's greatest teller of fairytales.

WORK SHEET 38

# Pronouns

**Reflexive pronouns are formed by adding –self or –selves to some of the personal pronoun forms. Relative pronouns are words that relate to a noun preceding it.**

## 1 Fill in the blanks with suitable personal or reflexive pronouns.

*a* _______ have not eaten anything since the morning.

*b* _______ fanned _______ with the newspaper.

*c* I found ______ hiding under the bed.

*d* I waved out to _______ but _______ did not wave out to _______.

*e* My father taught ________ to drive.

*f* After we bathed Jimmy, our dog, _________ ran to the garden and shook ________ dry.

*g* The baby tried to crawl by _______.

*h* The people saved _________ by jumping from the balcony.

*i* Aren't you ashamed of ________?

*j* "Save________," said the captain. "Jump out of the ship. _______ is sinking."

*k* The kitten put ______ sooty footprints everywhere.

*l* He put _______ finger on the buzzer and pressed hard.

*m* They went out in the wind to fly ________ kites.

*n* Please hand it back to Sally. It's _______.

## 2 Fill in the blanks with relative pronouns.

*a* I lost the book ________ you presented to me.

*b* They arranged the flowers ______ she received from her friend.

*c* The teacher called out for Shyam _______ quickly got up to collect his book.

*d* She is the girl ______ is known for her honestly.

*e* Pick up the toys _______ you have left on the floor.

# Interrogative Pronouns

**Some pronouns are used to ask questions, such as:**
Who? Which? What? Whose? Whom?

## 1 Answer these questions.

*a* What do you like for breakfast? ____________________

*b* Who is your favourite actor? ____________________

*c* Whose house is next door to yours? ____________________

*d* Which TV show do you like best? ____________________

## 2 Now it's your turn. Write four questions and ask a friend to answer them.

*a* Who ____________________?
____________________

*b* Which ____________________?
____________________

*c* What ____________________?
____________________

*d* Whose ____________________?
____________________

## 3 Fill in the missing pronouns to complete the questions.

*a* ________ is going with you to the football game on Sunday?

*b* ________ is the way to get to the skateboard park?

*c* ________ shoes were left on the school ground?

*d* ________ do you like to do on weekends?

## 4 Unscramble these questions. Remember to use question marks.

*a* gold lost a this Who watch morning ____________________

*b* socks lying the are dirty floor Whose on ____________________

*c* birthday your What you like for would ____________________

*d* bench with Who sitting park the on was you ____________________

*e* is to coast it Which way the ____________________

# Pronouns - Cohesive Ties

**Pronouns refer backwards and forwards to people and things. They tie ideas together.**

1 **One pronoun has been underlined. What noun does it replace?**

*a* "Will <u>you</u> make cakes for the school fete?" Sabina asked her mum. ____________

*b* Tina pointed to her brother and said, "I think <u>he</u> will win today." ____________

*c* "Will you let <u>me</u> have just one more turn, please?" asked Manav. ____________

*d* "Let <u>us</u> make a salad," said Dinesh to his friend. ____________

*e* Leena gave me the book and said, "Please put <u>it</u> on the shelf." ____________

2 **Pronouns usually refer backwards to a person or thing that has already been mentioned. Underline the pronouns. Draw an arrow back to the 'things' to which they refer.**

*a* The hikers, with backpacks on their backs, climbed steadily to the base camp of Mt Everest. The mountain towered above them. It looked impossible for them to climb.

*b* Sandeep and his two brothers joined the crowd that lined the streets of New Delhi for the Republic Day parade. They came to honour the memory of their grandfather. He had been a freedom fighter.

*c* Molly was a collector. She collected all kinds of frogs— big and little. She had glass frogs and stuffed frogs. She had plastic frogs, cloth frogs and clay frogs. She even had painted wooden frogs. Her father often could not understand it at all. Can you?

*d* The plane took off in light rain. The passengers sat back in their seats for take-off, with their seat belts fastened. The plane was soon in the air. It climbed rapidly and within fifteen minutes, it was cruising at very high altitude. A flight attendant walked down the aisle. She handed headphones or magazines to each passenger.

# Pronouns - Cohesive Ties

**Pronouns are an important feature of narrative writing. They tie ideas together. They constantly refer backwards and forwards, to people and things.**

**1 Highlight the pronouns. Draw an arrow back to the things they refer to.**

Peter Sox was thirsty. He really wanted a cup of tea. He had been out in his hot tin shed all morning, straightening the weather vane. The red tin rooster on top had screeched to a halt one windy Saturday back in May. It had refused to move after that. Peter entered the kitchen through the screen door. It squeaked in protest. "I need to grease that," he thought, "but a cup of tea is what I need just now."

**2 Continue the story by adding in the missing pronouns.**

Bobbie Sox looked up when Peter entered the kitchen. _______ noticed the grease under _______ fingernails. "_______'ve been greasing the gate ... again!" Bobbie Sox grimaced. _______ went back to _______ scribbling at the kitchen table.

Peter realised that if _______ wanted a cup of tea, _______ would have to get _______ himself!

**Personal pronouns are NOT used in information reports. Reports describe facts from an impersonal point of view.**

**3 Read the extract from a report on gold. Write an observation about pronouns.**

The discovery of gold in California in 1849, and in Australia in 1851, gave wealth to these young nations and led to population growth, new industries and improved transport and communication. The most famous goldfields in the world were discovered in 1886 in South Africa. Now the world's largest producer of gold, South Africa controls the price of gold on world markets.

**Observation:**

_______________________________________________

_______________________________________________

# Revision 2

1 Identify whether an interrogative adjective (A) or an interrogative pronoun (P) is used in the following sentences.

*a* Which programme do you like to watch? ________

*b* What time is the bus likely to leave? ________

*c* Which is your bag? ________

*d* Whose pencil is missing? ________

2 Identify the kind of adverb—manner (M), time (T) and place (P) in the following sentences.

*a* He waited angrily for his children to return. ________

*b* I want you to close the window immediately. ________

*c* We have looked for her everywhere. ________

*d* She is yet to return the library book. ________

*e* We all laughed heartily at the joker's antics. ________

*f* They accidently broke the window. ________

3 Write the antonyms of the following adverbs.

*a* nowhere ________

*b* strongly ________

*c* gently ________

*d* politely ________

*e* brightly ________

*f* gracefully ________

4 Frame questions using interrogative adverbs.

*a* We celebrate Gandhi Jayanti on 2nd October. ________

*b* The Eiffel Tower is in Paris. ________

*c* I went to play golf on Tuesday. ________

*d* She went to school by bus. ________

5 Write pronouns in place of the underlined nouns.

*a* <u>Shyam and Neena</u> enjoy watching plays. ________

*b* <u>The plant</u> is a rare one. ________

*c* <u>The monkey</u> is trying to snatch the banana from Seema. ________

*d* <u>My uncle</u> is the best tennis player. ________

# Revision 2

6 **Fill in appropriate reflexive/emphatic pronouns.**

*a* Though the food was not tasty, we forced ________ to eat it.

*b* They found _________ in a difficult situation.

*c* She excused ________ from the class.

*d* John hurt __________ when he fell down. He then got up by _________.

*e* She polishes her shoes __________.

*f* We insisted on paying the bill __________.

7 **Read the following paragraph and complete the table.**

Both my parents work in a bank. My father is full of energy and new ideas. He loves to take us out to new places on weekends and is always ready to play games with us. He can beat a clown in making faces. He can really make us laugh. Mummy is slim, serious and writes stories in her spare time. She always tells us a new story at bedtime.

| Adjectives | Adverbs | Pronouns | Verbs |
|---|---|---|---|
| | | | |

8 **Use arrows to show which nouns are replaced by pronouns.**

*a* Joe couldn't read the sign because it was too far away.

*b* Billy and Raj built a treehouse in their backyard.

*c* I help dad in the shed by handing him the tools he needs.

*d* Ms Basu frowned at Jyoti, so she put her pen down right away.

*e* "Do you want to come to the library with me?" Rohit asked Preeti.

9 **Fill in the blanks with suitable articles.**

*a* The children had seen ______ elf in the garden.

*b* Have you seen ______ five-legged dog?

*c* Mr Malhotra is _______ best teacher in our school.

*d* My sister would like to be ________ doctor when she grows up.

*e* Is this ______ book you lost?

# Prepositions

A preposition is a word in a sentence that tells us about the time and position. Prepositions generally come before nouns/pronouns. Words, such as under, into, between, towards, tell us about the position of the first noun in relation to the second nouns. They answer the question, 'Where is it?'

For example: The monkey jumped **from** the tree.
The picnic will be held **in** the garden.
The lunar eclipse will be seen **at** midnight.

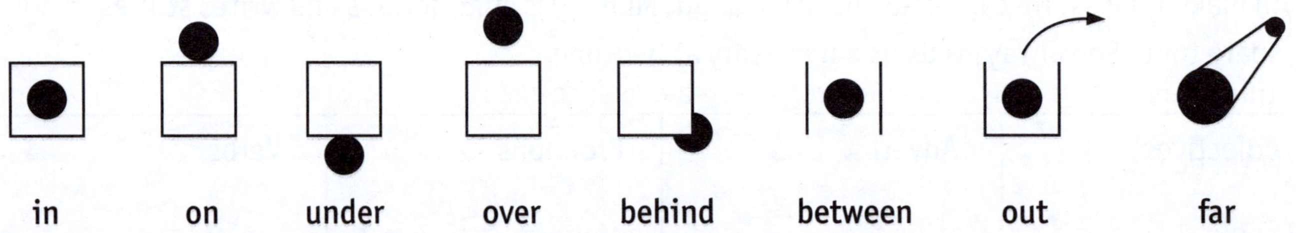


Prepositions, such as **on**, **at**, **by**, **for**, **since**, **past**, tell us when something happened. They answer the question **when** and are known as prepositions of time.

For example: We will keep awake **till** she comes.
It is **past** my sleeping time.

**Prepositions of purpose** are those that tell us about the use/purpose of something.

For example: On my birthday I decorated my room **with** streamers and balloons.
Please buy a dress **for** me.

**Prepositions of direction** tell us the direction—from, through, toward, across, to.

For example: The soldiers charged **towards** the enemy.
The rocket travelled **through** space.
They walked **around** the shopping centre.

Sometimes prepositions do the work of adverbs. They are called **adverbial prepositions.**

For example: You have eaten at this restaurant **before.**
We sat **near** the crying baby.

WORK SHEET 42

# Prepositions

**Preposition are little words whose job is to tell us about the position of someone or something.**

## 1 Choose the correct prepositions to fill in the blanks.

*a* He parked his car ________ the van ________ the cinema.

(beside, with, opposite)

*b* Those who are ________ eighteen cannot take part ______ the competition.

(for, in, above)

*c* The driver drove ________ the curve ________ full speed.

(at, down, round)

*d* I think it is ________ 6°C. I could do ______ a cup of coffee.

(with, below, of)

*e* I could swim ________ that pond ________ a few minutes.

(at, across, in)

*f* One can see ______ glass.

(through, at, below)

*g* Do not lean ________ the wall. It has just been painted ________ the contractor.

(with, by, across, against)

*h* She will not go ________ her mother ______ the market as it is ________ the road.

(to, without, between, across)

*i* Bake the muffins ________ a hot oven.

(with, in)

WORK SHEET 43

# Prepositions

**Prepositions are words that mean almost nothing on their own but have the important job of positioning people and objects in space.**

**1 Answer the following questions using suitable prepositions. The questions will give you a hint.**

*a* What are you waiting for?

______________________________

*b* What do we brush our teeth with?

______________________________

*c* Who jumped in the pool?

______________________________

*d* Where have you come from?

______________________________

*e* Since when have you been fishing?

______________________________

*f* Who was sitting near the statue?

______________________________

*g* What can you see behind the mountain?

______________________________

*h* Whose flat is below yours?

______________________________

WORK SHEET 44

# Prepositions

**A preposition introduces a phrase, a group of words containing a noun or pronoun, but no verb.**

## 1 Add a preposition to complete each phrase.

*a* Did you look ______ the cupboard _______ the missing sock?

*b* Dad bought a packet _____ golf balls ______ the sports store.

*c* She wrapped a ribbon ______ the parcel and tied it _______ a bow.

*d* My dog likes to trot _______ me when I go walking ______ the beach.

*e* ______ night, owls search _____ food.

## 2 Fill in the blanks to complete the passage.

I am Sunil and I live _____ Delhi. ______ summer I planned _____ travel to Shimla, because _____ the weather there. I took a train _____ Delhi to Kalka. _____ the railway station we went to our hotel ____ a car. We stopped _____ a small restaurant ____ a quick meal. The driver parked the car ______ the restaurant. Nobody could find the car and the driver, so we waited _______ the restaurant ______ one hour. The driver was walking _______ the small park ______ the restaurant, which we did not know of. We were very angry _______ him. But my holidays were great. I sat _______ campfires every evening and went _______ walks in the morning.

# Conjunctions

- Conjunctions are joining words. They join ideas together in a meaningful way.

**Coordinating conjunctions** include: *and, but, for, yet, so, or, nor*

- Coordinating conjunctions join words that are the same.
  For example: NOUNS Jack **and** Jill; tea **or** coffee; money **for** lunch
  ADJECTIVES tired **but** happy; ripe **and** juicy; yellow **or** orange
  ADVERBS here **and** there; fast **or** slow; quickly **but** carefully
  PRONOUNS she **and** I; us **or** them; no-one **but** me
- Coordinating conjunctions join phrases.
  For example: Sunita went up the steps **and** into the house.
  They battled across the raging river **and** up the steep, slippery bank.
- Coordinating conjunctions join simple sentences. These become compound sentences.
  For example: Rajan is leaving now **but** he'll be back later.
  Rohini is going to Melbourne **and** I'm going with her.
  It is getting dark, **so** I'll walk home with you.

**Correlative conjunctions** include: *whether ... or, both ... and, as ... as, either ... or, neither ... nor, not ... but, not only ... but also*

- Correlative conjunctions are used in pairs.
  For example: I can't decide **whether** to go to the skate park **or** to the movies.
  **Both** Anita **and** Tara left early. I will come **as** soon **as** I can.

**Subordinating conjunctions** include: *after, as, although, before, once, because, then, though, therefore, until, unless, where, wherever, when, whenever, while*

- Subordinating conjunctions are used to link a subordinate clause to a principal clause.
  For example: She was late **because** she lost her way.
  I will wait **until** my friends arrive.
  **When** the lights went out, we lit a candle.
  I'll look after the animals **while** you're away.

WORK SHEET 45

# Conjunctions

**Conjunctions are joining or link words. They include: and, but, so, or, yet, until, if, because, though, for.**

## 1 Underline the conjunctions in each of the following sentences.

*a* Although he was sick, he entertained the children.

*b* The cake came out well whereas the caramel custard was a disaster.

*c* I will go to church while you are in the mall.

*d* She may not recover unless there is a miracle.

*e* I will come to your house provided that you do not work too hard in the kitchen.

*f* As soon as she left, I went to the kitchen.

*g* He is unwell, still he plans to go to work.

*h* She is gentle, therefore everyone loves her.

## 2 All the missing conjunctions are hidden in the grid. Find them and fill in the blanks.

*a* They ate ______ drank.

*b* He will be here on Monday ______ Tuesday.

*c* She is small ______ strong.

*d* I was tired ______ I went to sleep.

*e* He will eat ______ he gets back.

*f* Jyoti had to go to the doctor __________ she was not feeling well.

*g* The visitors complained loudly about the heat, ______ they continued to play golf every day.

| | | | | | | | | | |
|---|---|---|---|---|---|---|---|---|---|
| E | Y | H | E | K | W | R | Q | T | W |
| O | H | E | J | A | S | W | H | E | N |
| R | H | R | M | N | D | T | A | G | G |
| D | J | T | K | D | S | H | Z | S | O |
| C | I | Y | L | E | F | K | S | Y | Y |
| F | B | U | T | T | G | M | D | U | H |
| G | L | G | U | T | B | N | F | J | G |
| C | B | E | C | A | U | S | E | N | F |
| T | J | F | T | G | H | C | Y | E | T |
| D | U | D | S | C | Y | I | O | O | L |

WORK SHEET 46

# Conjunctions

**Some conjunctions are used in pairs such as either-or, neither-nor, not only-but also. These are called correlative conjunctions. For example:**
Neither you nor Rohit can go out of the house.

## 1 Fill in the blanks using correlative conjunctions.

*a* He is ____________ intelligent ____________ good-natured.

*b* I will ____________ go for a walk ____________ for a swim.

*c* He is ____________ rich ____________ famous.

*d* ____________ did he do his homework ____________ did he study for the test.

*e* She is ____________ clever, ____________ hard-working.

*f* She turned ____________ to the right ____________ to the left.

*g* It is ____________ ____________ hot, ____________ ____________ humid.

## 2 Make sentences using appropriate words from columns A, B and C.

| A | B | C |
|---|---|---|
| Raman did not eat or drink | but | the others have to be dry cleaned. |
| Some dresses can be washed | nor | peas are winter vegetables. |
| We will watch the movie | and | he was unwell. |
| Neither Gaurav | if | Mona came for the party. |
| Carrots | because | We get the tickets. |

______________________________________________

______________________________________________

______________________________________________

______________________________________________

______________________________________________

# Sentences

A sentence is a group of words that make sense. A sentence must at least have one verb. A sentence begins with a capital letter and ends with a full stop, question or exclamation mark.

**Simple sentences** have two parts — a subject and a predicate, which contains the verb.

| Little Bo-Peep | lost her sheep. |
|---|---|
| Subject | Predicate (with the verb) |
| | |
| Bobby | climbed the tree. |
| Subject | Predicate |

**Compound sentences** consist of two simple sentences joined by a co-ordinate conjunction—and, but, so, yet, or.

For example: Jake drove the car **and** Mary red the map.
I'd like to go to the football game, **but** I don't have a ticket.
Jane is coming over, **so** we can play chess.
Would you like to read, **or** do you want to play cricket?

**Complex sentences** are made up of a main (principal) clause and one that depends on it (subordinate).

A **clause** is a group of words that forms part of a sentence and has a subject and predicate.

The **subordinate clause** begins with a relative pronoun (who, which, whom, that) or a subordinate conjunction. The subordinate clause can be placed at the beginning, or embedded in the middle and is separated from the rest of the sentence by commas. Common conjunctions include: though, although, after, as, before, because, since, then, once, until, unless, where, wherever, when, whenever, while.

Speech marks are used around spoken words in dialogue.

For example: "Dinner at seven o'clock," called Mum.
"What are we having?" Jose replied.

**Paragraphs** consist of any number of sentences, grouped around a single main idea.

**Connectives** are words used to sequence ideas across text.

For example: last Sunday, first, then, soon, afterwards, suddenly

# Sentences

**A sentence begins with a capital letter and ends with a full stop, question mark or exclamation mark.**

## 1 Locate the sentences. Use capital letters and full stops.

Alchemists lived in the Middle Ages they were not very good scientists and often relied on magic rather than careful study alchemists dreamed of changing cheap metal into gold they tried to make a magic substance which they called the 'philosopher's stone' they said this would cure diseases and keep people young however no stone ever appeared and alchemists fell into disrepute

## 2 Underline the subject in each sentence.

*a* The first known Olympic contest was held in 776 BC in southwest Greece.
*b* In October 1970, the West Gate Bridge collapsed in a pile of steel and concrete.
*c* Learning to roller skate is not an easy thing to do.
*d* By the time he was eighteen, Grant Kenny had won eight Iron Man titles.
*e* Hawaii may have the best surf in the world, but Australia has the best surfers.

## 3 Write a sentence and a question about each subject.

A tiger ______________________

______________________

Lightning ______________________

______________________

A compass ______________________

______________________

Oil ______________________

______________________

WORK SHEET 48

# Sentences – Subject and Predicate

**Sentences have two parts:**
- **the subject – the person or thing the sentence is about;**
- **the predicate – what is written about the subject.**

**The predicate always includes the verb.**

**The small plane** | ***flew*** **low over the mountains.**

The SUBJECT — The PREDICATE

**1 Put a box around the subject of each sentence.**
**Observe where subjects are placed in sentences.**

*a* An exploding volcano often sends out a cloud of poisonous gases.

*b* A cold front is the leading edge of a moving mass of cold air.

*c* Faster and faster, the skier sped down the mountain slope.

*d* From all over the world came messages of sympathy.

*e* At the factory, pineapples are processed and canned.

*f* In no time at all, Julie had finished reading her book.

Observation: ______________________________

**A simple sentence has only one subject and one verb.**
**A singular subject has a singular verb. A plural subject has a plural verb.**
**For example:** The player **is wearing** a red jersey and blue shorts.
The players in the team **are wearing** red jerseys and blue shorts.

**2 Write simple sentences using these subjects:**

| | | |
|---|---|---|
| *the Indian flag* | *a flash of lightning* | *the stricken plane* |
| *honeybees* | *the heavy drawbridge* | *a large, beautiful rose garden* |

*a* ______________________________

*b* ______________________________

*c* ______________________________

*d* ______________________________

*e* ______________________________

*f* ______________________________

WORK SHEET 49

# Affrmative and Negative Sentences

**A sentence with 'no' or 'not' is a negative sentence. A sentence without a 'no' or 'not' is a positive sentence. A positive sentence is also called an affirmative or declaratory sentence. For example:** I am going out now. **An example of a negative sentence:** It is not raining today.

**1 Read the following sentences and identify the positive (P) and negative (N) sentences.**

*a* All of us are leaving tonight. ______

*b* We were not planning to go out today. ______

*c* I hope you enjoyed your stay in our house. ______

*d* The tigers are rarely seen. ______

*e* Nobody is reading me this book. ______

*f* None of the girls want to play outdoors. ______

**2 Change the following affirmative sentences to negative sentences and the negative sentences to affirmative sentences.**

*a* The teacher is very busy.

______

*b* They are very helpful.

______

*c* Nobody in our family can dance.

______

*d* Shyam and Ram don't eat vegetarian food.

______

*e* They did all the work by themselves.

______

*f* She isn't interested in going out.

______

*h* He wasn't feeling well to play with us.

______

*i* My father drives carefully.

______

*j* I believe in miracles.

______

*k* The children ate all the cheese in the box.

______

# Compound Sentences

**A compound sentence is made up of two or more simple sentences joined by a conjunction. For example:** I bought apples and Jane bought figs. Ram likes bananas, but his sister likes guavas. It is wet, therefore I can't play outside.

## 1 Join the two sentences, using these conjunctions:

| *and* | *but* | *so* | *yet* | *or* |
|---|---|---|---|---|

*a* Payal has an appointment at three o'clock, _____ she must leave early.

*b* I would like to buy this violin, _____ it is too expensive.

*c* I am going to Thailand _____ I'd like you to come with me.

*d* She went away for a very long time, _____ she never forgot us.

*e* Would you like orange juice, _____ would you prefer lemonade?

## 2 Add a second sentence to make a compound sentence.

*a* Tarun gazed through the telescope and ______________________________.

*b* My friend gave me a dollar, but ______________________________.

*c* I needed a haircut, so ______________________________.

*d* Did you buy a new T-shirt, or ______________________________.

*e* He knew the forest well, yet ______________________________.

**Simple sentences can be joined by a conjunction, or separated by a comma, to make a compound sentence. For example:** Tina wants to go swimming, Mia would rather play tennis and Jo wants to play cards.

## 3 Join the sentences to make a compound sentence.

*a* Dark storm clouds gathered in the west. Thunder rolled across the sky.

______________________________

*b* It was late at night. The weather remained warm and humid.

______________________________

*c* Tom collects stamps. Jerry sketches birds. Bill doesn't have a hobby.

______________________________

WORK SHEET 51

# Compound Sentences

**Two simple sentences, joined together, make a compound sentence. For example:** I bought apples and Jaya bought figs. Ram likes bananas, but his sister likes guavas.

Joining words are called *conjunctions*. Some joining words are: **and, but** and **so.**

## 1 Join the two sentences, using these conjunctions:

| *and* | *but* | *so* |
|---|---|---|

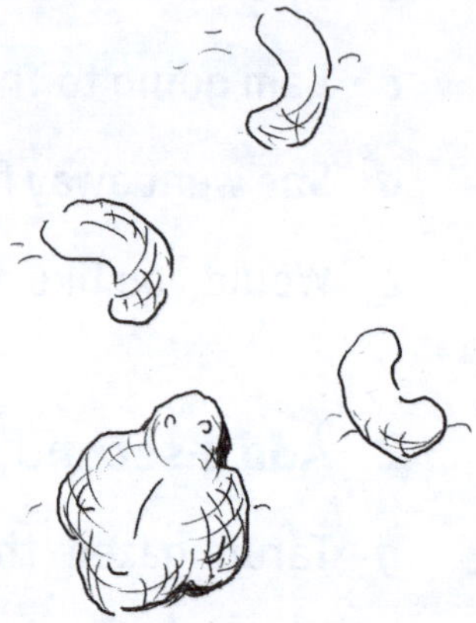

*a* I am hungry, ______ I will eat lunch.

*b* He wanted to go, ______ his dad wouldn't let him.

*c* She called his name, ______ he didn't hear her.

*d* Pia likes jelly beans ______ she likes chocolate frogs.

*e* There's enough room in our car, ______ you can come with us.

## 2 Add your own sentence to make a compound sentence.

*a* Jack played tennis and ____________________________________.

*b* I eat lettuce, but ____________________________________.

*c* Sumit wanted a pet bird, so ____________________________________.

## 3 Join the two sentences with a conjunction.

| | | | |
|---|---|---|---|
| *a* | Tom wants to go in the pool | *and* | you may go home. |
| *b* | Mia has black hair | | the tank is full. |
| *c* | The bell has rung | *so* | I also like tea. |
| *d* | Gagan knocked at the door | | he can't swim. |
| *e* | I like coffee | *but* | Sarah is blonde. |
| *f* | It rained heavily | | no one answered. |

# Complex Sentences

**A complex sentence is made up of a principal clause and a subordinate clause. They can be joined by a conjunction. For example:** Put your scraps in the bin when <u>you have finished eating.</u>

| | |
|---|---|
| A subordinate clause can be at the **beginning**, → | *Before it gets too late,* I will catch a bus home. |
| in the **middle** or at → | The car, *because it is new,* is clean and shiny. |
| the **end** of a sentence. → | The dams will be full *when the drought ends.* |

## 1 Put a box around the principal clauses.

*a* Kartik was unhappy because he had lost his football.

*b* As we walked across the street, a car came rushing round the corner.

*c* When you are ready, we will go to the park.

*d* While I was at the beach, I collected a bucket of shells.

*e* The audience went home after the concert was over.

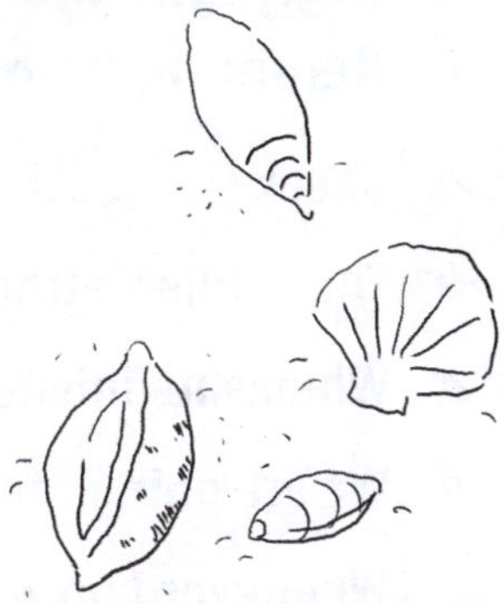

A comma is needed after a subordinate clause **at the beginning** of a sentence.

## 2 Highlight the subordinate clauses.

*a* Did Monica tell you where she was going?

*b* We won't be in the final, because we didn't win our last game.

*c* Stand there until I tell you to move.

*d* Although he is only small, he is very strong.

*e* I must get home before the sun goes down.

## 3 Complete the sentences by adding a subordinate clause.

*a* It started to rain, so ________________________________.

*b* When ____________________________, they hid behind a large rock.

*c* We go to our music lesson then ____________________________.

*d* Because ____________________________, the driver went very fast.

# Complex Sentences

**A complex sentence is made up of a principal clause and a subordinate clause. They can be joined by a conjunction. For example:** Put your scraps in the bin when you have finished eating.

| A subordinate clause can be at the **beginning** or at the **end** of a sentence, or it can be embedded in the **middle.** | ***Before we left for Agra***, *we checked the map.*<br>*The car,* ***because it is new***, *is quiet and reliable.*<br>*Our water tanks will be full* ***when the drought breaks.*** |
|---|---|

**1 Highlight the principal clauses.**
**Remember a main idea may be interrupted by an embedded clause.**

*a* Check the depth of the pool before you dive in.
*b* The soldier, although he was wounded, struggled back to camp.
*c* When she finished reading her book, she returned it to the library.
*d* We are going camping this weekend unless it rains.
*e* Whenever I go walking, my dog, Rusty, comes with me.
*f* I will make the beds while you cook breakfast.

**2 Highlight the subordinate clauses. They may appear at the beginning, in the middle or at the end of a sentence.**

*a* Diamonds are very valuable because they are rare, hard and beautiful.
*b* Deserts become very cold when the sun disappears in the afternoon.
*c* When the Ganges flooded in 1974, many properties were destroyed.
*d* Beetles keep their thin wings folded unless they are flying.
*e* The first books, as far as anyone knows, were made in Egypt 5000 years ago.
*f* Not many adults ride bicycles although they are an easy form of transport.

**3 Complete the sentences by adding a subordinate clause.**

*a* It started to rain before ______________________________.
*b* When ______________________________, the bird flew away in fright.
*c* I go to my training session then ______________________________.
*d* Because ______________________________, I had to stand in the rain.

WORK SHEET 54

# Complex Sentences

**A complex sentence is made up of a principal clause and a subordinate clause. They can be joined by a relative pronoun. For example:**
She is a person who is very fond of animals.
This is the costume that I will wear on stage.

I'll use **which** and **that** to talk about animals and things.

I'll use **who** to talk about people.

## 1 Complete the subordinate clauses.

*a* A botanist is a person who ________________________________.

*b* I have a book, which ________________________________.

*c* A sports coach is one who ________________________________.

*d* I want you to know that ________________________________.

*e* You'll never guess who ________________________________!

*f* This is my new watch, which ________________________________.

*g* It is a problem that ________________________________.

Use a comma before *which* but not before *that*.

## 2 Use **which**, **that** or **who** to fill the gaps.

*a* Is this the chess piece __________ you lost?

*b* Picasso painted many pictures, __________ are now famous.

*c* I am sure __________ all my answers are correct.

*d* Mozart was a composer __________ wrote many wonderful pieces of music.

*e* I made a big chocolate cake, __________ everyone enjoyed.

*f* Alexander Bell, __________ was born in Scotland, invented the telephone.

*g* In the middle of the forest, there was a house __________ looked like a castle.

*h* Rumaan Kidwai was a musician __________ was nicknamed 'The Wild Sarangi Boy'.

WORK SHEET 55

# Complex Sentences

**A complex sentence is made up of a principal clause and a subordinate clause. They can be joined by a relative pronoun.**

## 1 Complete the subordinate clauses.

*a* A doctor is a person who ____________________.

*b* I have a book, which ____________________.

*c* These are the boys who ____________________.

*d* I want you to know that ____________________.

*e* You'll never guess who ____________________!

*f* This is my new bike, which ____________________.

## 2 Use which, that or who to fill the gaps.

*a* A pilot is a person __________ flies planes.

*b* Here is your hat, __________ you left in the playground.

*c* This is the picture __________ I have been painting.

*d* It was a song __________ everybody was singing.

*e* This is my book, __________ you may like to read.

*f* The townspeople cheered the men __________ had put out the fire.

WORK SHEET 56

# Sentences - Paragraphs

**A paragraph is a block of sentences built around one main idea.**
**A paragraph begins with an idea or topic and the following sentences add details.**

Paragraphs can be separated by a line space OR by indenting the first line. As a general guideline, paragraphs have at least two sentences, but no more than ten.

**Here is an example:.**
Antarctica is the coldest, highest, windiest, loneliest continent on Earth. It is bigger than Australia, but almost no one lives there. Much of the continent remains unexplored.

The South Pole is in the middle of Antarctica. This region has very long winters where the sun may not rise for months. The winters are the coldest on Earth...

**1 Divide this extract from a report on the eclectus parrot into paragraphs. Draw a line around each paragraph, or use different highlighters.**

The eclectus parrot is unique among the many species of parrot. Unlike other parrots, both the male and the female have brilliantly coloured plumage. This parrot is large and stocky with a short squat tail and long round-tipped wings. The male is brilliant green with bend of wing blue. The underwing and sides of his body are red. The female is mostly bright red with a blue-purple lower breast. Eclectus parrots live in the canopy of forests in New Guinea. They extend west to the Moluccas, east to the Solomon Islands and south to the tip of Cape York in Australia. They nest in hollows in fig, milkwood and black bean trees. Their nest hollows can be 20 to 30 metres above the ground. The female eclectus parrot almost never leaves the vicinity of her nest, relying on the male birds to bring her food. If disturbed, she flies off with raucous cries to a nearby tree, but returns as soon as it is safe. Even when the chicks are fledged, she continues to return and jealously guard her nest. Eclectus parrots live on a diet of fruit, seeds, leaf buds, blossoms and nectar. A number of male parrots feed the female at the nest entrance, and she in turn, feeds her chicks. The female lays two eggs in spring. Eggs hatch in about 30 days and the chicks leave the nest around 3 months. Many chicks are lost to predators, especially pythons, or are drowned when heavy rain fills the nest hollow. In the past eclectus parrots have fallen victim to poachers and the lucrative bird-smuggling trade. The near extinction of these beautiful birds has been prevented because of laws for the protection of wildlife, and the successful breeding of these parrots in captivity. Research continues into the complex social systems and the breeding habits of the wild eclectus parrot.

**2 Write two paragraphs about two of the following items. You will need to say what each looks like and what it does. You may choose to illustrate.**

a *hot air balloon* a *windmill* a *suspension bridge* a *parachute*

WORK SHEET 57

# Sentences in Dialogue

**Sentences can record the speech of one person to another. This is called dialogue. Speech marks are placed around the spoken words. For example:**
"I went to Jaipur last holidays," said Kartik.
"Was it hot there?" asked Rohit.

**1 Using a different colour for each speaker, highlight the spoken words in this dialogue. Note the placement of the speech marks.**

"What can you tell me about the moon?" asked the teacher.
"It is a satellite of the Earth," said Raj immediately.
Sarah added, "It is our nearest neighbour."
"And it is much smaller than the Earth," said Mukul.
The teacher then asked, "What do people see when they look at the full moon?"
Raj said, "The face of a man."
"A girl reading a book," said Sarah.
Mukul laughed, "Sometimes they see a jumping rabbit."
"And sometimes they see an old man with a bundle of sticks on his back," added the teacher, smiling.

Spoken words are separated from unspoken words by a comma, question mark or exclamation mark. Note their placement. The first spoken word has a capital letter. Each new speaker is given a new line.

Speech can be written in **present**, **past** or **future** tense.

**2 Punctuate these questions and answers.**

- Highlight the spoken words.
- Put speech marks around the spoken words.
- Give the first spoken word a capital letter.
- Separate the spoken words from the unspoken words.

*a* Will you sponsor me in the Walk against Want asked Todd
Yes said Mrs Jiggs I'll give you Rs 2 per kilometre

*b* Have you read the latest Gordon Black novel asked Pia
No sighed Gautam I haven't been able to buy a copy anywhere

*c* Did you win your hockey game Ronit asked
No, the Punjab Devils won by one point said Sandeep sadly

# Punctuation

| | |
|---|---|
| **Capital letters are used for:** | |
| • the first word in a sentence. | *Come to the circus with me.* |
| • proper names. | *Cinderella danced with Prince Charming.* |
| • the first spoken word in dialogue. | *He said, "Let's play cricket."* |
| • to emphasise important words. | *You did WHAT?* |
| **Full stops** end statements and commands. | *That is a fine straw hat.*<br>*Put it on, please.* |
| **Question marks** end questions. | *How long will you be away?* |
| **Exclamation marks** end exclamations. | *What! Late again!* |
| **Commas are used:** | |
| • to separate words in a list. | *I like apples, pears, plums and grapes.* |
| • to separate a beginning phrase. | *Later that day, we went for a swim.* |
| • to separate a beginning clause. | *When I broke my leg, I used crutches.* |
| • to separate an embedded phrase. | *Jassi, waving her umbrella,*<br>*hurried away.* |
| • to separate an embedded clause. | *My dog, which is old now,*<br>*still does tricks.* |
| • to separate spoken and unspoken words. | *"A dingo is a wild dog," said Bradley.* |
| **Speech marks** are used around spoken words.<br>***Remember: NEW speaker NEW line.*** | *"Dinner is on the table," called Brinda.*<br>*"Thank you," Jassi replied.*<br>*"Me too!" shouted Joy.* |
| **Apostrophes are used:** | |
| • with nouns to show possession. | *Joel's toys; dog's collar;*<br>*teachers' staffroom* |
| • to contract pronouns and helping verbs. | *I've packed lunch. You're invited.*<br>*It's fun.* |
| • to contract helping verbs and negatives. | *He can't swim. I couldn't sing.*<br>*Don't shout.* |
| **A colon is used:** | |
| • after a character's name in a script. | *THE GIANT: You thief! Come back!*<br>*JACK: Come on big guy! Catch me!* |
| • to introduce a list of items.<br>(A bullet point often precedes each item.) | *You will need to bring:*<br>• *a raincoat*<br>• *stout walking shoes*<br>• *extra food* |

# Punctuation

**1 Insert punctuation marks (commas, full stops, question marks, exclamation marks and apostrophes) in the correct places.**

*a* The farmer has goats ducks cows pigs and chickens
*b* My neighbours dog bites strangers
*c* "Ah Ive done it at last" said Rohit
*d* As I was walking towards the market I met my friend
*e* What a rude man he is said my aunt in anger
*f* "Long ago" said the teacher "there lived an old man in a castle in the town of Pench
*g* I bought a book a box of pencils my sister bought a writing pad an album and a ruler
*h* "Whos that" asked Neha
*i* Mr Das who is a good painter lives near my house
*j* One evening I was sitting with Mickey in the hall we saw a man walking with a camel on the road
*k* The guard found his masters wallet in the ladies toilet
*l* "Isnt she ready yet" asked my uncle "shes never on time"

**2 Punctuate this short dialogue.**

Why are you boys so late in coming back to class the teacher asked
Ben replied we were in the library and didn't hear the bell

**3 Punctuate the following text.**

Mozart was born in Austria two hundred and fifty years ago he was a clever little boy and soon learned to play the piano he wrote many wonderful pieces of music many people believe Mozart to be the greatest composer who has ever lived.

# Similes, Metaphors and Idioms

How are similes and metaphors different?

A **simile** explains the comparison and begins with words such as **like**, **as**, **as if** and **as though**.

For example: as sweet as sugar tells us that what we are talking about has the quality of sweetness (like sugar).

**Metaphors** also make comparisons in a different way from similes. They only hint at the comparison and leave you to work it out yourself.

For example: Annie flew downstairs.

What are we comparing Annie with? We are comparing Annie with a bird.

How is she like a bird?

A bird moves quickly.

My father towered over us.

This means that my father is so tall that he can be compared to a tower.

**Idioms** are also expressions similar to metaphors.

For example: to get into hot water means getting into trouble.

Read the following idioms and their meanings.

| | |
|---|---|
| To be under the cloud | to be under suspicion |
| To burry the hatchet | to settle a quarrel and live in peace |
| To be a wet blanket | to be a spoilsport |
| To draw the long bow | to exaggerate |
| To take the bull by the horns | to accept challenges boldly |
| To show the white feather | to show cowardice |
| To flog a dead horse | to do work which produces no results |
| To be a dog in the manger | to deny to others what is useless |
| To be a clean breast of it | to confess to some wrong |
| To have an axe to grind | to have something to gain by an action |

WORK SHEET 59

# Similes, Metaphors and Idioms

**Similes, metaphors and idioms are phrases that describe by making comparisons.**

## 1 Look at the pictures and complete the following similes.

*a* As brave as a __________ 

*b* As busy as a __________ 

*c* As cool as a __________ 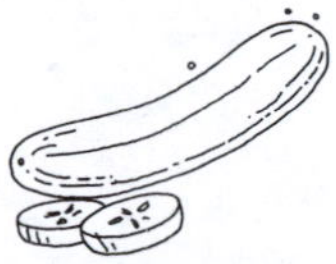

*d* As green as __________ 

*e* As light as a __________ 

*f* As heavy as __________ 

*g* As fast as a __________ 

*h* As fresh as a __________ 

## 2 Fill in the blanks using the above similes.

*a* Rita was as ______________________________ helping her father clean the cupboards.

*b* Rohit woke up early morning feeling as ______________________________.

*c* Each soldier in the platoon was as ______________________________.

*d* He never gets angry; he is always as ______________________________.

*e* He ran as ______________________________ and came first in the race.

*f* She opened her report card with a heart as ______________________________.

# Similes, Metaphors and Idioms

**Similes, metaphors and idioms are phrases that describe by making comparisons.**

**1 In the sentences below underline the metaphors, explain what is being compared in each and how the two things are alike.**

*a* The clouds sailed across the sky. ____________________

*b* We ducked down out of sight. ____________________

*c* My teacher exploded when I gave the reason of my absence. ____________________

*d* She skimmed through the book. ____________________

*e* They wolfed down their lunch in a minute. ____________________

**2 Frame sentences using the following metaphors.**

Striking when the iron is hot.
Turning over a new leaf.
Letting the cat out of the bag.

____________________

____________________

____________________

____________________

**3 Choose the correct idiom.**

*a* Yes, tell me about it. I'm **all ears.**

Listening carefully ☐

Listening quickly ☐

*b* Well, he's not that at all. He's **a bird brain.**

A fool ☐

A criminal ☐

# Similes, Metaphors and Idioms

**Similes, metaphors and idioms are phrases that describe by making comparisons.**

*c* You mean he's **a bad egg?**

A stupid person ☐

A dishonest person ☐

*d* I was so upset with the quality of the machine that I went round to his shop **like a bull in a china shop** in the show room.

Shouting at him ☐

Knocking everything over ☐

*e* Roma got her money back and as a result she **opened up a whole new can of worms** because other people got their money back, too.

Discovered some creatures on the carpet ☐

Exposed a lot of serious problems ☐

**4 Given below is a list of common idioms. Choose the correct option to fill in the blanks.**

*a* Make a ____________ out of a molehill.

*b* Blow your own ____________.

*c* A ____________ stone gathers no moss.

*d* A bird in ____________ is worth two in a bush.

*e* The ball is in your ____________.

*f* Call a spade a ____________.

*g* The early bird catches the ____________.

| *court* | *mountain* |
|---|---|
| *spade* | *rolling* |
| *trumpet* | *hand* |
| *worm* | |

# Phrases

A phrase is a group of words without a verb or subject, often beginning with a preposition. Phrases add meaning and detail to sentences.

For example: They are walking in the park.
They are walking along the beach.
They are walking to get some fresh air.

Phrases are groups of words that give language its rhythmical flair. Jack and Jill went out their back door, up the hill, and over the top, down the lane, into the park, up the tree and over the fence, into the barn, among the cows, through the paddock, in front of the fence, behind the gate ... and sat under the apple tree.

Different phrases have different jobs to do.

**Prepositional phrases** begin with a preposition.

For example: **into** the park, **over** the road, **beside** the creek, **under** the tank stand, **up** the ladder, **around** the bend

**Adjectival phrases** answer the question which. They do the same work as adjectives. They can begin with a:

- Preposition
  A boy **with red hair** walked past the window.
- A present participle
  The diver, **wearing a wet suit,** slipped into the sea.
- A past participle
  We found a rabbit **abandoned on** the street.
- An infinitive
  I got a message **to wait here.**

**Noun phrases** answer the question what. They do the same work as nouns.

For example: **Walking every** day is good exercise.
I like **climbing trees.**

# Phrases

**Adverbial phrases** do the same work as adverbs. There are four types of adverbial phrases:

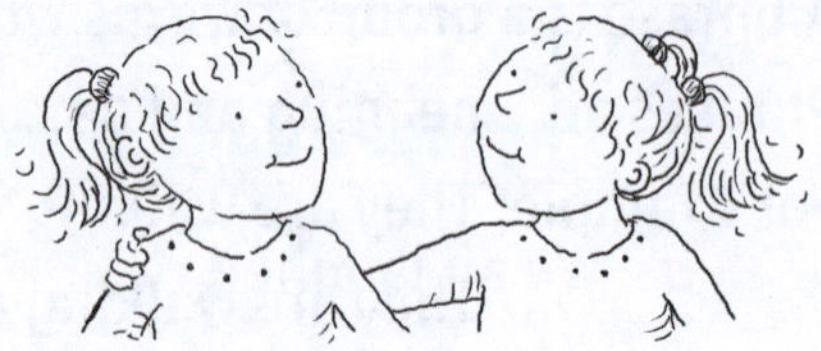

- TIME (when?)
  For example: I met my friends **after school.**
- PLACE (where?)
  For example: Put the box **on the table.**
  The cat is **under my chair.**
- MANNER (how?)
  For example: He pushed **with all his strength.**
  She waited **with great patience.**
- REASON (why?)
  For example: The game was stopped **because of rain.**
  They worked hard to **earn some money.**

# Phrases

**A phrase is a group of words within a sentence.**
**For example:** out the door, up the tree, into our cubby, off to school.

A phrase has NO verb.
It adds important information to a sentence.

## 1 Phrases add important information. Join these phrases so they make sense.

| | |
|---|---|
| *a* We all laughed | for you. |
| *b* I only took one apple | under a tree. |
| *c* She has been waiting | with me. |
| *d* He shared the chocolate | at the clown. |
| *e* The tired farmer sat | from the bowl. |

## 2 Time to sketch. The phrases will help you know what to do.

| | | |
|---|---|---|
| A frog is sitting <ins>on a log</ins>. 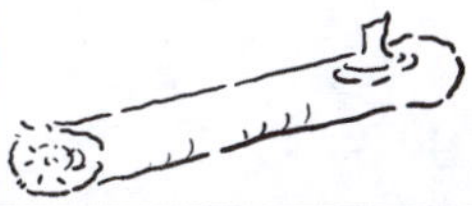 | I am standing <ins>under an umbrella</ins>.  | Dad went <ins>up the ladder</ins>.  |
| The cup fell <ins>off the table</ins>. 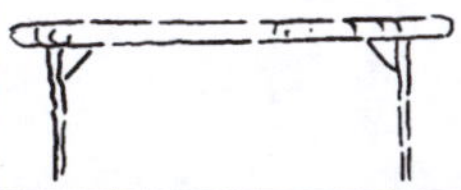 | A duck walks <ins>towards the lake</ins>.  | There's a dog <ins>beside the chair</ins>.  |

## 3 Circle the phrases in red.

*a* The kitten hid under the rocking chair.

*b* At home, we often play Monopoly.

*c* The clock on the wall has stopped ticking.

*d* A big band marched down the street.

*e* Last night, we saw the full moon in the sky.

*f* Our car in the garage has a flat tyre.

*g* The runners jogged around the lake.

WORK SHEET 62

# Phrases

**A phrase is a group of words within a sentence. The group has NO verb. For example:** in the library; on the shelf; at the skate park; after the disco; off to sleep.

## 1 Phrases add important information. Join the parts to make sense.

| | |
|---|---|
| ***a*** The weary sailors returned | in the blink of an eye. |
| ***b*** There were severe water restrictions | in such polluted water. |
| ***c*** The meteor disappeared | on the walls of the cave. |
| ***d*** There are ancient rock paintings | after months at sea. |
| ***e*** You will not be able to swim | during the drought. |

## 2 Write three possible phrases to complete the sentences.

***a*** The hot air balloon floated ____________________.
____________________.
____________________.

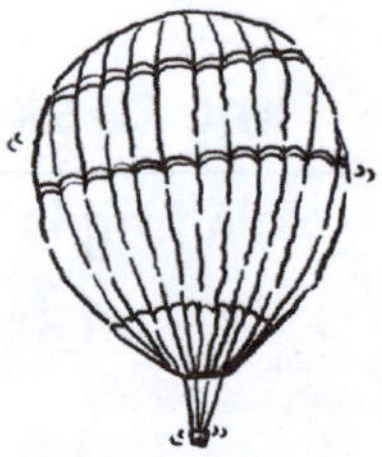

***b*** An old man ____________________ walked past our gate.
____________________
____________________

***c*** Wild horses thundered ____________________.
____________________.
____________________.

***d*** ____________________ there are many wild creatures.
____________________
____________________

WORK SHEET 63

# Noun Phrases

**Noun phrases do the same work as nouns. For example:**
Walking every day is good exercise. I like climbing trees.

Noun phrases can be the **subject** of a sentence.
For example: *Playing the piano* is great fun.
Noun phrases can be the **object** of a sentence.
For example: I like *walking my dog*.

**1 Highlight the noun phrases in these sentences.**

*a* We wanted to go swimming on Sunday.

*b* Being school captain was her greatest dream.

*c* Seeing you there was such a surprise.

*d* We must learn to care for each other.

*e* Riding skateboards is not allowed here!

**2 Select a noun phrase to complete each sentence.**

| | | |
|---|---|---|
| *climbing Mt Everest* | *to fly solo* | *leaving all my friends* |
| *to get home* | *growing orchids* | *waiting patiently* |

*a* Mr Gupta enjoys ______________________________ in his greenhouse.

*b* ________________________________________ was really sad.

*c* Jayant wanted ______________________________ before nightfall.

*d* ______________________________ is hard when you are really excited.

*e* ________________________ was Sir Edmund Hilary's greatest achievement.

*f* Smithy's dream was __________________________ across the Tasman Sea.

**3 Write four sentences using these noun phrases:**
*playing the violin* *eating popcorn* *to sing a song* *flying kites*

________________________________________

________________________________________

________________________________________

________________________________________

WORK SHEET 64

# Adjectival Phrases

**Adjectival phrases do the same work as adjectives. For example:** the girl with blue eyes; a box of chocolates; the bird in the cage. **They can begin with prepositions, participles or infinitives. For example:** the boy in the blue cap; the boy wearing a blue cap; a message to wear a blue cap.

**1 The adjectival phrases have been underlined. Circle the nouns they describe. Note the position of the adjectival phrase.**

*a* The shoes in the box are new and expensive.

*b* The boy riding that horse is only six years old.

*c* She handed the note from her mother to the teacher.

*d* Mr Mehta is proud of the flowering orchids in his greenhouse.

*e* At the corner shop, we bought two packets of potato chips.

*f* The students, dressed in school uniform, arrived at the history museum.

**2 Choose an adjectival phrase to complete each sentence.**

*a* At the picnic we shared a plate ____________________.

*b* Her gift was in a box ____________________.

*c* The leaves ____________________ are crisp and brown.

*d* Lily finally decided to buy the dress ____________________.

*e* The jockeys, ____________________, lined their horses up at the barrier.

*f* Little Miss Tina, ____________________, stepped out onto the stage.

| | | |
|---|---|---|
| *wearing colourful silks* | *tied with silver ribbon* | *wearing a brave smile* |
| *of buttered corn* | *beneath our feet* | *with sequins round the hem* |

**3 Don't misplace adjectival phrases. Rewrite these sentences correctly.**

*a* The students went to see the elephants wearing their broad-brimmed hats.

____________________________________________

*b* The boys were a menace to the walkers riding around in the park.

____________________________________________

*c* The tourists with their webbed feet enjoyed seeing the platypuses.

____________________________________________

WORK SHEET 65

# Adjectival Phrases

**Adjectival phrases do the same work as adjectives.**
**For example:** the girl with blue eyes; the horse in the paddock; the cup on the saucer.

**1 The adjectival phrases have been underlined. Circle the nouns they describe.**

*a* Please wash the cups in the sink.

*b* He chose the chocolate in the gold wrapper.

*c* The man with sunburnt skin is a farmer.

*d* Will you help me carry this box of books?

*e* The bell above the door is made of brass.

**2 Link the adjectival phrase to the noun it describes.**

| | | |
|---|---|---|
| *a* | The curtains | in the jug |
| *b* | The vase | under the bed |
| *c* | The dog | over the window |
| *d* | The water | on the table |
| *e* | The cat | with the flea collar |

**3 Now use each noun and phrase from above in sentences of your own.**

*a* ____________________________________________

*b* ____________________________________________

*c* ____________________________________________

*d* ____________________________________________

*e* ____________________________________________

# Adverbial Phrases

**Adverbial phrases do the same work as adverbs.**
**For example:** He ran across the road. Wait until Friday. He walked with long strides.

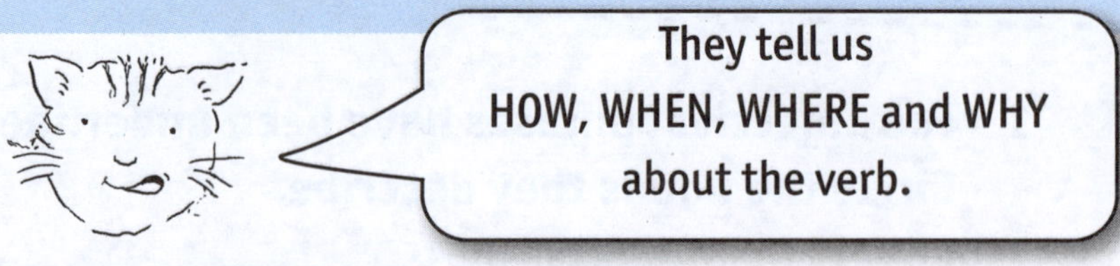


## 1 Do the adverbial phrases say HOW, WHEN, WHERE or WHY?

*a* *Before school* we have singing practice. __________

*b* Lean your bike *against the wall.* __________

*c* He spoke *in a soft voice.* __________

*d* Thank you *for your help.* __________

*e* *In thirty seconds* the alarm will ring. __________

*f* The soldier was given a medal *for his bravery.* __________

## 2 Complete the sentences by choosing an adverbial phrase from the box.

| | | |
|---|---|---|
| *into the pool* | *during the storm* | *in ten minutes* |
| *with a soft cloth* | *for your sister* | *on the stove* |
| *below the waves* | *after the party* | *under a log* |

*a* He polished his shoes ______________________. *(how)*

*b* The train will depart ______________________. *(when)*

*c* ______________________ dived a spear fisherman. *(where)*

*d* Take another apple ______________________. *(why)*

*e* ______________________ branches broke like matchsticks. *(when)*

## 3 Write sentences using these adverbial phrases.

*a* along the sandy beach *b* through the open window *c* between the bookshelves

*a* ______________________________________________

*b* ______________________________________________

*c* ______________________________________________

# Adverbial Phrases

**Adverbial phrases do the same work as adverbs.**
**For example:** He ran past the gate. The sun set in the west. She arrived home before dark.

## 1 Do the adverbial phrases say HOW, WHEN, WHERE or WHY?

*a* Ferries chug <u>across the brown, slow-flowing river</u>. __________

*b* I need fifty rupees <u>for a ticket</u> to the football game. __________

*c* <u>Without fear</u>, the skier set off down the mountain. __________

*d* There was little or no rain <u>during April</u>. __________

*e* Wait <u>for me</u>! __________

*f* They dived <u>beneath the waves</u> in search of the wrecked ship. __________

*g* The sale will continue <u>until 30 June</u>. __________

*h* On Christmas morning, I woke up <u>in great excitement</u>. __________

## 2 Add the missing adverbs or adverbial phrases.

During the holidays, I like to go (where) ______________________________.

It is a busy, bustling place (where) ______________________________.

There are hundreds of tiny stalls, selling food, clothing, books and jewellery (how) ______________________________. It is a colourful, noisy exciting place.

I like to collect old coins. I look (where) ______________________ for them.

(when)______________________, I'm lucky and find a stall tucked away (where) ______________________. Often the stall keeper has some rare old coins (where) ______________________ on his table. Unfortunately, I can seldom afford to buy any. However, I can usually pick up an old penny or a foreign coin (why) ______________________.

| | | |
|---|---|---|
| *everywhere* | *in a corner somewhere* | *in a glass case* |
| *to the marketplace* | *near the main railway station* | *sometimes* |
| *to add to my collection* | *at bargain prices* | |

# Clauses

- A **clause** is a group of words with a subject and a verb.
  For example: *Dad and I went fishing.*
  *The athlete won a blue ribbon.*

- A **principal clause** contains the main idea.
  A simple sentence has just <u>one</u> principal clause.
  For example: *Bill likes watching action movies.*
  *Birds fly home at sunset.*

- A **subordinate clause** can be placed at the beginning, the middle (embedded clause) or at the end of a sentence. A clause at the beginning, or embedded in the middle, is separated from the rest of the sentence by commas.
  For example: I will get out of bed *when the sun rises.*
  *When the sun rises,* I will get out of bed.
  If you call me, *when the sun rises,* I will get out of bed.

- A subordinate clause is joined to the principal clause by a **conjunction** or a **relative pronoun.**
  For example: *She was late* (principal) ***because*** *she lost her way.* (subordinate)
  *This is the house* (principal) ***that*** *Jack built.* (subordinate)

- These are the **relative pronouns** we use to join clauses:
  *who, whom* (used when talking about people)
  *which, that* (used when talking about things)

These are the **conjunctions** we most often use to join clauses:

| | | | | |
|---|---|---|---|---|
| *after* | *because* | *or* | *though* | *whenever* |
| *although* | *before* | *so* | *unless* | *where* |
| *and* | *but* | *then* | *until* | *wherever* |
| *as* | *once* | *therefore* | *when* | *while* |

WORK SHEET 68

# Noun Clauses

**Many subordinate clauses do the work of nouns. They are called noun clauses. Noun clauses usually tell what someone is thinking, saying or feeling. For example:** He asked what time it was. They once believed that the world was flat.

## 1 Highlight the noun clauses in these sentences.

*a* He found it hard to believe that Gauri was a champion horse rider.

*b* I don't know when I'll be back.

*c* You can tell I've never done this before!

*d* After I won a trophy at the swimming competition, Dad said he was proud of me.

*e* We couldn't tell who was leading the great cycle race.

*f* The boys in the rowing team think they will win their race on Saturday.

## 2 Complete the sentences using noun clauses. Tip: Ask the question WHAT?

*a* I thought ______________________________

*b* No one could guess ______________________________

*c* Do you know ______________________________

*d* I smiled when Samir said ______________________________

*e* He pretended ______________________________

## 3 Locate the seven noun clauses in this account.

The night of the school concert arrived. Our senior choir opened the show. Amit, who was a great singer, was next. You could tell he was feeling very nervous. However, he sang well and the audience clapped loudly. Later he said that he had relaxed once he was out on stage. Soon it was my turn. I stepped onto the stage to play a lively piece on the piano. I had been practising for weeks and I felt that I knew it well. Seated at the piano, I sensed that everyone's eyes were on me. Nevertheless I played my best. The audience cheered and Mohit said that he didn't know I could play so well. The concert finished with our massed choirs. Mr Govind said that we had all performed very well. He said we should feel very proud of ourselves.

WORK SHEET 69

# Adjectival Clauses

**Many subordinate clauses do the work of adjectives. They are called adjectival clauses. For example:**

Bell is the man who invented the telephone.

It was a meteor that flashed across the sky.

I'll use **which** and **that** to talk about animals and things.

I'll use **who** to talk about people.

Adjectival clauses always follow the they describe.

**1 Underline the noun or pronoun that the adjectival clause describes.**

*a* The planet, *which has just been discovered*, may contain life.

*b* A geologist is a person *who studies rocks*.

*c* It is an invention *that could change the way we shop*.

*d* All the tourists *who visit Prague* agree that it is a wonderful old city.

*e* He discovered a fossil, *which the museum could not identify*.

*f* The refugees, *who had queued for several hours*, finally received a bag of rice.

*g* Mr Kishore picked all the peaches *that were ripe*.

**2 Add who, which or that to complete the clauses.**

*a* The replay showed the player ________ had been injured during the tackle.

*b* Chris washed all the clothes ________ he had worn at the school camp.

*c* I didn't know the person ________ knocked on the door.

*d* The cave, ________ we discovered by accident, was small, dark and musty.

*e* There is the clock, ________ is known throughout the world as .

*f* This is just one of the many castles ________ overlook the Danube River.

**3 Use who, which or that in sentences of your own.**

*a* ____________________________________________

*b* ____________________________________________

*c* ____________________________________________

WORK SHEET 70

# Adjectival Clauses

**Many subordinate clauses do the work of adjectives. They are called adjectival clauses.**
**For example:** She is a person who likes animals.
I am buying the game that was advertised on TV.

I'll use and to talk about animals and things.

I'll use **who** to talk about people.

Adjectival clauses always follow the **noun** they describe.

## 1 Underline the noun or pronoun that the adjectival clause describes.

*a* The horse, which he bought for Rs 10,000, became a great racehorse.

*b* Everyone who could sing, joined the choir.

*c* He gave her a necklace that was made of gold and diamonds.

*d* The people, who had been waiting for a long time, were pleased to see the train.

*e* An hour before the shop closed, all the meat that was left was reduced in price.

## 2 Add **who**, **which** or **that** to complete the clauses.

*a* The movie showed the men __________ first landed on the moon.

*b* The cattle dog, __________ is now very old, rounded up all the stray cows.

*c* This is the treehouse __________ took us two weeks to build.

*d* I didn't know the person __________ knocked on the door.

*e* We visited the zoo to see the polar bear __________ had just been born.

## 3 Use **who**, **which** or **that** in sentences of your own.

*a* ____________________________________________

*b* ____________________________________________

*c* ____________________________________________

WORK SHEET 71

# Adverbial Clauses

**Many subordinate clauses do the work of adverbs. They are called adverbial clauses. For example:**

He went to bed because he was very tired.

I will buy a football when I have enough money.

Adverbial clauses tell us more about the verb.
They tell us:
*How Where When Why*

**Conjunctions** link them to the principal clause.

## 1 Note what the adverbial clauses tell us – how, when, where or why.

*a* The astronauts needed oxygen tanks *while they were on the moon.* ______

*b* The guide showed us a cave *where we saw wonderful cave paintings.* ______

*c* *After I do all my research on fungi,* I will table my information. ______

*d* We sat round the campfire *because it was so cold.* ______

*e* I will come *as fast as I can.* ______

*f* Once we're at the shopping mall, you may go *wherever you wish.* ______

*g* *Although an emu has wings,* it cannot fly. ______

*h* I am not going *unless you come with me.* ______

*i* People could not cross rivers and seas *until they invented boats.* ______

*j* *When gold was discovered,* many people made their fortune. ______

## 2 Write the conjunctions from the sentences above. Then search them out in the box.

______

______

______

______

______

______

______

______

______

______

| | | | | | | | | | |
|---|---|---|---|---|---|---|---|---|---|
| S | F | P | T | N | C | J | O | K | R |
| D | W | H | E | R | E | V | E | R | B |
| Y | H | G | Y | P | F | Q | I | H | D |
| U | E | B | E | C | A | U | S | E | E |
| U | N | L | E | S | S | I | R | U | R |
| E | T | I | E | L | T | E | E | O | E |
| L | I | T | H | Q | R | T | T | R | H |
| I | F | N | E | P | O | W | F | J | W |
| H | G | U | O | H | T | L | A | P | Y |
| W | L | O | W | X | S | H | S | A | D |

WORK SHEET 72

# Adverbial Clauses

**Many subordinate clauses do the work of adverbs. They are called adverbial clauses. For example:**

He went to bed because he was very tired.
I will buy a football when I have enough money.

Adverbial clauses tell us more about the verb.
They tell us:
*How Where When Why*

**Conjunctions** link them to the principal clause.
You will find a list of conjunctions on the first page of this lesson.

## 1 Note what the adverbial clauses tell us – how, when, where or why.

*a* I will make the toast, while Dad cooks the eggs. ____________

*b* Nandita knows a great spot where we can have a picnic. ____________

*c* After I get dressed for school, I will make my lunch. ____________

*d* You can't go in because you haven't got a ticket. ____________

*e* I will come as fast as I can. ____________

*f* My dog follows me wherever I go. ____________

*g* Although she played well, she was not picked for the team. ____________

*h* I am not going unless you come with me. ____________

*i* We cheered until all the players left the field. ____________

*j* When the tide goes out, we will pick up shells on the sand. ____________

## 2 Write the conjunctions from the above sentences. Then search them out in the box.

____________
____________
____________
____________
____________
____________
____________
____________
____________
____________

| | | | | | | | | | |
|---|---|---|---|---|---|---|---|---|---|
| S | F | P | T | N | C | J | O | K | R |
| D | W | H | E | R | E | V | E | R | B |
| Y | H | G | Y | P | F | Q | I | H | D |
| U | E | B | E | C | A | U | S | E | E |
| U | N | L | E | S | S | I | R | U | R |
| E | T | I | E | L | T | E | E | O | E |
| L | I | T | H | Q | R | T | T | R | H |
| I | F | N | E | P | O | W | F | J | W |
| H | G | U | O | H | T | L | A | P | Y |
| W | L | O | W | X | S | H | S | A | D |

# Adverbial Clauses

**Adverbial clauses tell us more about the verb in a sentence. Conjunctions link them to the principal clause. For example:** Joe stood up so the old lady could sit down. I will come to the party when I have finished netball training.

**1 Highlight the adverbial clauses. Circle the conjunctions.**

*a* The man did not speak until everyone was quiet.

*b* When I broke my leg, I had to use crutches.

*c* Don't play in the sun unless you wear a hat.

*d* You must think before you speak.

*e* Our class went to the library then to the pool.

*f* Mum said I couldn't go because I was too young.

*g* Whenever you can come, I will be happy to see you.

*h* I'll stay here while you get your school bag.

**2 Write the conjunctions given below in the empty boxes.**

*a* I'll eat the soup [ ] it is hot.

*b* [ ] you go to the shop, will you get me a dozen eggs?

*c* We couldn't see [ ] the lights went out.

*d* Simon knows a place [ ] we can pitch our tent.

*e* [ ] he hurt his knee, he continued to play the game.

| although | after | where | before |
|---|---|---|---|
| while | unless | because | when |

# Prefixes and Suffixes

A **prefix** (affix) is a word, or letter(s) placed at the beginning of another word (a base word) to adjust or qualify its usage or meaning. The opposite of prefix is suffix.

Sometimes adding a prefix, such as **un-**, **in-**, **dis-**, **im-**, to a word can make it into an antonym.

For example: un + sure = unsure

im + possible = impossible

dis + please = displease

in + action = inaction

Other prefixes, such as **ir-**, **ill-**, **il-**, **non-**, also make antonyms.

For example: il + legal = illegal

non + resident = non-resident

**Suffixes** are letter(s) placed at the end of the word to form a new word.

Nouns become plurals by adding **–s**, **-es**, **-en.**

For example: tree: trees

box: boxes

- Tenses of verbs change by adding **–s**, **-es**, **-d**, **-ed.**
  For example: eat: eats
  place: placed
- Adjectives become adverbs by adding **–ly.**
  For example: sad: sadly
- Sometimes a verb becomes a noun by adding a suffix.
  For example: teach : teacher
- When a word ends with **e**, we add only **–s.**
  For example: house: houses
- When a word ends with **y** we change the **y** to **i** and add **–er.**
  For example: happy : happier
- -**Ful** and -**ness** are also suffixes. They can make a verb change to an adjective.
  For example: harm: harmful
  home: homeless

WORK SHEET 74

# Prefixes and Suffixes

**Suffixes and prefixes change, adjust or modify the meaning of the word they are attached to.**

**1 Fill in the blanks by adding prefixes to the words in the brackets.**

*a* He is __________ of what is happening around him. (aware)

*b* The __________ from USA are here on a holiday. (migrants)

*c* The pain in his arm is __________. (bearable)

*d* Her handwriting is ________ (legible)

*e* You think it is _________ for me to do this work. (possible)

*f* He may not have gone to school but we can't call him _________ because he educated himself at home. (educate)

*g* Mahatma Gandhi started the ________________ movement. (cooperation)

*h* Please ___________ the wires. (connect)

*i* The painting was kept in the sun, it is looking __________. (coloured)

**2 Fill in the blanks by adding suffixes to the words given in the brackets.**

*a* The __________ the test, the ___________ is the marking. (easy, tough)

*b* Is Mt Everest the __________ mountain in the world? (high)

*c* He is very __________ because he is always in a hurry. (care)

*d* A mosquito is the _________ of malaria and other diseases. (carry)

*e* She is always ________ with a smile on her face. (cheer)

*f* The ______ on the horse is also a __________. (ride, teach)

*g* The floods left many people __________. (home)

*h* Look at that __________ painting. (beauty)

*i* He ran so fast the we became ____________. (breath)

*j* The Patels are _____________ people and excellent hosts. (wonder)

# Composition

## Writing a Story

Do you like to read stories? Have you ever written a story on your own.
Remember the following rules of writing a story:

- The story should have a title.
- A story is generally written in past tense.
- The story should introduce and give names to characters.
- A story should be interesting.
- A story has direct speech, interjections and contractions.
- A story has a well-developed plot—mystery, adventure, comedy.
- The contents of the story should match the title.
- A story can be developed from an introduction or a beginning.
  Her face lit up when she saw ...
  ... it was nothing but a dream.

**1 Create a short story using the outline given below.**

Beggar child on road – person in car – takes him home – looks after him – admits him to a school – boy grows up – become doctor – looks after his aged adopter.

WORK SHEET 76

# Composition

## Writing a Story

**2 Write a story about one of the following.**

Bow Wow

My grandmother

Up the mountain

# Composition

## Writing a Story

**1 Write a story of your choice. Start the story with any one of the following:**

"I don't believe it!"

The day I dropped food on the new carpet ...

That day I opened the door to a stranger ...

# Composition

## Paragraph Writing

The purpose of any paragraph is to express an idea. Most paragraphs consist of a few related sentences.

Before you start writing a paragraph, you need to answer two questions. What are you writing about? What do you want to say?

The key to writing a paragraph is to break down the writing into short, simple steps.

Remember the rules:

- Keep the sentences short and simple.
- Keep the topic/theme in mind.
- Sentences should have nouns, adjectives, adverbs and the other parts of speech to make the paragraph interesting.
- The first sentence tells us about what we are writing about and the last sentence concludes the paragraph.

For example: if one were to write a paragraph on a dog, one could follow the following framework.
Animal – domestic – features – breed – colours – characteristics – qualities – pet dog – protector – loyal

**1 Write a paragraph based on the above framework.**

# Composition

## Paragraph Writing

**1 Write a paragraph on any one of the following.**

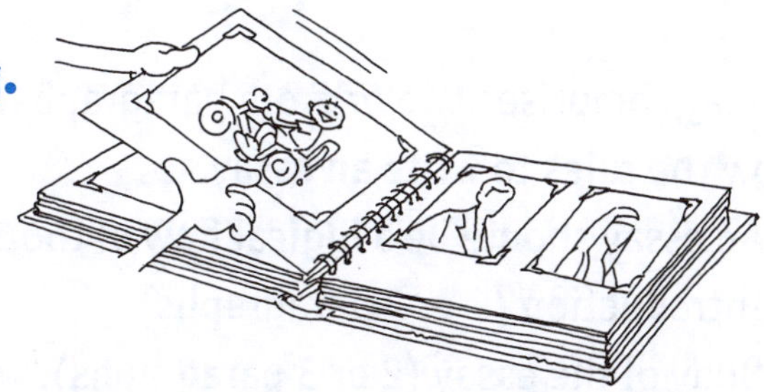

My family album

Birthday presents

My first ride on a bicycle

# Composition

## Essay Writing

An essay comprises two or more paragraphs.

Follow the rules to write an essay.

- An essay should be a logical flow of thoughts.
- Introduction (1 or 2 paragraphs)
- Body of the essay (2 or 3 paragraphs), which include description, what happens, how it happens, why.
- Essays in general are written in present/past tense.
- Good use of dialogue in the right places makes the essay interesting.
- The conclusion should not be abrupt.

**1 Write an essay on any one of the following. A basic framework has been provided.**

Introduction – Taj Mahal – location– structure – construction – garden - history – world heritage site – tourism

Conclusion – why I like/not like the Taj Mahal

# Composition

## Essay Writing

# Composition

Essay Writing

## 1 My favourite festival

Introduction – name – month – season

Body – what people do – why it is celebrated – how it is celebrated in my family

Conclusion – other festivals – why I enjoy celebrating this festival.

# Composition

## Notice Writing

On your trip to the zoo, did you come across some notices?

| DO NOT FEED THE ANIMALS |
|---|

| DO NOT TEASE THE ANIMALS |
|---|

| DO NOT TOUCH THE ANIMALS |
|---|

Notices are brief. They serve as guidelines for us to follow for our safety. They are generally written in big, bold letters and displayed at prominent places.

**1 Write a notice for any two of the following.**

On city roads
Outside the doctor's room
Outside your classroom
On hilly/mountainous roads

# Composition

## Message Writing

A message is a verbal, written or recorded communication sent by one person to another.
A message is brief and to the point.
A verbal message can be sent through a messenger or over the telephone.

Rohit: Meet me at the Central Park in Gol Market tomorrow at 4 p.m. (Message)
Mohit: Yes, I will! Give me the directions. (Acceptance of the message)

**1** **Imagine that you are the principal of the school. Write a message for the students.**

**2** **Send a message to your aunt informing her about your arrival. Mention the time, date and transport by which you will arrive.**

WORK SHEET 84

# Composition

## Book Review

Do you read books? Have you ever chosen to read a book after reading its review?
What is a book review?
A book review tells us what the book is about, why it should be read and the interesting features of the book.

### Tips on writing a book review:

- Give the title and the author of the book.
- Write an interesting introduction that makes the reader want to read on.
- Give a short outline about the plot (what happens) of the book.
- Write about your favourite part using adjectives.
- Provide an exciting ending without telling the reader the end of the book!

### Sample book review

The book I read: *The Wit of Tenali Raman* by Devika Rangachari

This book is a collection of eighteen short stories about Tenali Ramakrishna, popularly known as Tenali Rama. A jester at the court of King Krishna Devaraya, Tenali was the king's favourite and always managed to triumph over with his wit and intelligence. These humorous exploits of Tenali also show his concern for truth and a desire to bring to light the follies of people and society.

I would give it a silver star.

# Composition

**1 Try writing a book review using the following format.**

Book title:

Author:

The character I liked best:

What went wrong:

How the problem was solved:

The funniest part:

The saddest part:

The sort of reader who would like this book:

I would give it a gold/silver/bronze medal

# Revision 3

**1 Fill in the blanks with the appropriate prepositions (single word or group of words with a preposition). Remember prepositions generally come before a noun.**

*a* The tourist found himself ________ ________ a river and a forest.

*b* Students were shouting ________ ________ ________ of their voices.

*c* I stood ______ the speaker, so that I could hear him.

*d* She was looking ______ her book all _______ the house.

*e* The vase fell ______ my hand and broke _______ pieces.

**2 Use the following prepositions to make interrogative sentences.**
**to, from, except for, in spite of**

____________________________________________

____________________________________________

____________________________________________

____________________________________________

____________________________________________

**3 Fill in the most appropriate conjunctions in the sentences.**

*a* He could not understand physics, _________, he kept trying to learn it. (because, wherever, however)

*b* The gardener has to water the saplings ________he sows the seeds, _________ they will die. (while, after, otherwise, unless)

*c* Mr Goyal cut him short________ he was right. (and, although, but)

*d* Don't go near the monkey ________it may harm you. (if, but, because)

*e* She invited all her friends________ relations_______ left out Ravi; _______ he had once hit her. (because, for, and, when, but)

*f* He will cry ________ we do not return his toy. (if, or, for)

# Revision 3

**4 Rewrite the following sentences using appropriate conjunctions.**

*a* My mother was upset. She forgave me.

______________________________

*b* I was too busy playing. I forgot to complete my homework.

______________________________

*c* She was not invited. She did not come.

______________________________

*d* I shall come. It does not rain.

______________________________

*e* Rita may be in the house. Rita may be in the garden.

______________________________

*f* Raman failed in his test. He was idle.

______________________________

**5 Make sentences with the following conjunctions.**

Neither-nor ______________________________

Either-or ______________________________

Not only-but also ______________________________

**6 Underline the principal clauses in each of the following sentences.**

*a* She built a house where she could see the mountains.

*b* She bathed the child because he was dirty.

*c* I kept my books where I could find them.

*d* You may sleep wherever you like.

*e* You look tired as though you have not slept for a long time.

*f* He will do the work as you tell him to do it.

# Revision 3

**7 Circle the subordinate clauses.**

*a* Keep sitting on the chair till I tell you to get up.

*b* Did he tell you where his house is?

*c* Not many people travel by the Metro, although it is the cleanest and the fastest mode of transport.

*d* When I go for a walk, I wear warm clothes.

**8 Underline the phrases in the given sentences.**

*a* She will be here in a few minutes.

*b* You can buy this book in all the bookshops.

*c* The girl with brown eyes is my cousin.

*d* They placed their bags, full of toys, under the bed.

*e* The plants in the garden are exotic.

*f* The old man found it difficult to climb up the mountain wet with rain water.

**9 Identify the subject, verb and object from the above sentences**

| Subject | Verb | Object |
|---|---|---|
| *a* | | |
| *b* | | |
| *c* | | |
| *d* | | |
| *e* | | |
| *f* | | |

**10 Use the following phrases to make sentences.**

At the well ______________________________

Full of ripe fruit ______________________________

With great kindness ______________________________

Lit up the sky ______________________________

# Revision 3

**11** **Rewrite the sentences using contractions for the underlined words.**

*a* We will try our best.

*b* After I had eaten my dinner, I rested.

*c* She was not at the meeting.

*d* Has not the mail arrived?

*e* She cannot swim well.

*f* What is the matter with you?

**12** **Punctuate the following.**

*a* The manager said please come in

*b* Oh cried my sister I've hurt my finger

*c* long ago began the teacher there lived a king and a queen.

**13** **Look at the following pictures and write a short story or a poem.**

# WORD BANKS Antonyms

## Opposites

### ADJECTIVES

| | |
|---|---|
| awake | *asleep* |
| black | *white* |
| bright | *dull* |
| clean | *dirty* |
| cold | *hot* |
| dear | *cheap* |
| expensive | *cheap* |
| far | *near* |
| fast | *slow* |
| fat | *thin* |
| fat | *lean* |
| fresh | *stale* |
| full | *empty* |
| great | *small* |
| high | *low* |
| ill | *well* |
| kind | *unkind* |
| light | *dark* |
| light | *heavy* |
| little | *big* |
| long | *short* |
| old | *new* |
| old | *young* |
| right | *wrong* |
| right | *left* |
| sad | *happy* |
| small | *large* |
| smooth | *rough* |
| smooth | *coarse* |
| soft | *loud* |
| soft | *hard* |
| top | *bottom* |
| ugly | *beautiful* |
| wet | *dry* |
| wide | *narrow* |
| wild | *tame* |

### VERBS

| | | | |
|---|---|---|---|
| come | *go* | open | *close* |
| ebb | *flow* | sleep | *wake* |
| open | *shut* | stand | *sit* |
| sink | *float* | stop | *go* |
| throw | *catch* | win | *lose* |

### NOUNS

| | | | |
|---|---|---|---|
| day | *night* | dawn | *dusk* |
| love | *hate* | friend | *foe* |
| morning | *afternoon* | life | *death* |

### ADVERBS

| | | | |
|---|---|---|---|
| late | *early* | now | *then* |
| sooner | *later* | often | *seldom* |

### PREPOSITIONS

| | | | |
|---|---|---|---|
| above | *below* | behind | *ahead* |
| after | *before* | in | *out* |
| off | *on* | over | *under* |
| up | *down* | with | *without* |

# WORD BANKS Collective Nouns

a brood of chickens
a business of ferrets
a cete of badgers
a cloud of flies
a clowder of cats
a clutch of eggs
a flock of birds
a gaggle of geese
a herd of buffalo
a herd of elephants
a litter of cubs
a mob of cattle
a murder of crows
a pack of dogs
a rake of colts
a shoal of fish
a shrewdness of apes
a siege of herons
a skulk of foxes
a sloth of bears
a swarm of bees
an army of frogs

a bevy of quail
a convoy of trucks
a covey of partridges
a flock of sheep
a kindle of kittens
a leap of leopards
a mob of kangaroos
a pack of wolves
a parliament of owls
a pod of whales
a pride of lions
a rafter of turkeys
a school of porpoises
a smack of jellyfish
a string of racehorses
a team of horses
a tiding of magpies
a troop of monkeys
a warren of rabbits
a watch of nightingales
a wedge of swans
an exaltation of larks

# WORD BANKS Compound Words

afternoon
anthill
armchair
backside
bandstand
barnyard
baseball
basketball
bathroom
bedroom/ bedtime
bellboy
birthday
blackboard
bookcase
bookends
bookmark
bridegroom
broomstick
bulldozer
bullseye
buttercup
buttermilk
butterscotch
cardboard
carthorse
cartwheel
catfish
cornflakes
cowboy/ cowgirl
daybreak
daydream
daylight
daytime
dipstick
doorbell
doorknob/ doorknock
doorstep
doorstop
doorway
downhearted
downhill
downstairs
downstream
downtown
downtrodden
drainpipe
driveway

eggplant
eggshell
eyebrow
eyelash
eyeliner
failsafe
fairway
fairytale
farmland
farmyard
fingernail
fireball/ firefly
firelight/ fireplace
fireman/ firestorm
fireproof
foolhardy
football/ footman
footbridge/ footloose
footpath/ footprint
fullback
gentleman
goalkeeper
godmother/ godfather
grandmother/grandfather
grandstand
grapefruit
grapevine
halfback
handbag
handheld
handlebar
handmade
handstand
haystack
headlight/ headstand
heartbeat/ heartfelt
herself/ himself
hillside
homeland
homesick
homestead
horseback/ horseplay
horsehair/ horseshoe
hornpipe
houseboat
household
inland/ inlet

inside
jumpstart
junkyard
kickboxer
landslide/ landline
leeway
lifeline/ lifetime
lighthouse
lightweight
lunchbox
manhole
manpower
matchbox
matchstick
merry-go-round
milkman
milkshake
moonlight/ moonbeam
mothballs
mudpie
nevermore
nickname
nightdress
nightfall
night-time
nursemaid
offside
outpost
outside
overall
overeat
overleaf
overstay
overtime
paperweight
pathway
penknife
pickpocket
pigsty
pinwheel
playtime/ playhouse
policeman
popcorn
porthole
postcard
postman
pothole

quarterback
quarter-time
railway/ railroad
rainbow/ raindrops
raincoat
rosebud
sandbag
sandcastle
scarecrow
shockproof
shoelace/ shoestring
showtime
skylight
slipstream/ slipway
snowball/ snowflake
snowman
softball
starlight/ starburst
steamroller
stopwatch
sunbeam/ sunburst
sunlight/ sunshine
tablecloth
teapot
telltale
timeline
timepiece
toenail
toothpaste/ toothbrush
topside
towbar
toyshop
washstand
watchmaker
waterbed/ watermelon
watercolour/ waterway
watercourse/ waterproof
waterfront/ watercress
waterhole/ watertight
watermark / waterfall
waterworks
waxworks
weekend/ weekday
whirlwind
windmill
witchcraft

# WORD BANKS Gender

## masculine, feminine

*Gender refers to whether something is male, female or neither (neuter). Pronouns* he, his, him, she, her, hers, it *and* its *show the gender of someone or something in English. Some suffixes show whether something is male or female. Nowadays these suffixes tend not to be used with people, as they are considered to be sexist, for example* actor, actress; hero, heroine.

boar, sow
bull, cow
cob, swan
dog, bitch
drake, duck
fox, vixen
gander, goose
gentleman, lady
lion, lioness
man, woman
ram, ewe
rooster, hen
stag (or buck), doe
stallion, mare
steer, heifer
tiger, tigress

actor
author
aviator
baron, baroness
count, countess
duke, duchess
emperor, empress
hero
king, queen
lord, lady
poet
prince, princess
sir, dame
sir, madam
uncle, aunt
waiter, waitress

# WORD BANKS Homographs

words that are identical with another in spelling but different in meaning.

angle
arms
back
ball
bank
bar
bark
base
bat
bay
beam
bear
beat
bill
bit
blind
block
blow
board
booty
bow
brand
cape
case
cast
change
charge
chop
club
coach
coat
coast
cold
column
corn
count
court
craft
crane
cricket
crop
cross
crow
dock
down
draught
draw
drill
drive
drone
duck
express
fair
fast
felt
file
fill
fine
fire
fit
flag
fleet
float
fold
foot
form
game
gape
grain
grate
grave
ground
gum
hail
hamper
hand
hide
hit
hold
host
iron
jam
jar
joint
jumper
June
just
kid
kind
kite
lap
last
lay
lead
lean
leaves
left
let
letter
lie
lift
light
line
list
litter
lock
log
mail
march
mass
master
match
may
mean
might
mine
mint
mould
mount
nail
nature
note
order
organ
page
palm
pass
patient
peal
plot
plug
pole
port
post
pound
power
private
prune
pupil
race
range
rank
record
rent
rest
rifle
right
ring
rock
roll
rose
round
row
ruler
rung
sack
safe
save
scale
scales
seal
season
shed
sheet
sign
sink
smoke
soil
sound
sow
speaker
spell
spoke
spring
squash
staff
stage
stall
stand
star
state
steer
stern
stick
stock
stole
strike
stud
stump
suit
swallow
swift
table
tear
temper
tile
till
top
train
trip
tumbler
turn
vote
wake
watch
wave
well
wind
work
yawn

# WORD BANKS Homophones

ail / ale
air / heir
aisle / isle / I'll
allowed / aloud
alter / altar
arc / ark
arms / alms
ascent / assent
ate / eight
aunt / aren't
awe / or / oar / ore
bail / bale
bald / bawled
bare / bear
bark / barque
barren / baron
base / bass
be / bee
beach / beech
been / bean
beer / bier
bell / belle
berry / bury
birth / berth
bite / bight
blew / blue
boar / bore
board / bored
boarder / border
bold / bowled
born / borne
bough / bow
bow / beau
boy / buoy
braid / brayed
braise / brays
brake / break
bread / bred
brews / bruise
bridal / bridle
but / butt
buy / by / bye
cannon / canon
canvas / canvass
capital / capitol
carrot / carat
cast / caste
caw / core / corps
cede / seed
ceiling / sealingcellar /
seller
cent / scent / sent
centred / scented
cents / scents / sense
cereal / serial
cheap / cheep
check / cheque
chews / choose
choral / coral
cite / sight / site
clause / claws
coarse / course
coat / cote
colonel / kernel
council / counsel
creak / creek
crews / cruise
cue / queue
curb / kerb
currant / current
cygnet / signet
days / daze
dear / deer
dew / due
die / dye
died / dyed
dies / dyes
doe / dough
draft / draught
draw / drawer
dying / dyeing
earn / urn
ewe / you / yew
ewes / use
eye / I
eyelet / islet
faint / feint
fair / fare
farther / father
fate / fete
feat / feet
find / fined
fir / fur
flaw / floor
flea / flee
flew / flu / flue
flocks / phlox
flow / floe
flower / flour
for / fore / four fort /
fought
foul / fowl
frays / phrase
freeze / frieze
gait / gate
gamble / gambol
genes / jeans
gild / guild
gnaw / nor
gored / gourd
gorilla / guerrilla
grate / great
grater / greater
groan / grown
guest / guessed
hail / hale
hanger / hangar
hart / heart
heal / heel / he'll
hear / here
heard / herd
hears / here's
hew / hue
higher / hire
him / hymn
ho / hoe
hoard / horde
hoarse / horse
hose / hoes
hole / whole
holy / wholly
hour / our
idle / idol
in / inn
island / Ireland
jam / jamb
key / quay
knave / nave
knead / need / kneed
knew / new
knight / night
knot / not
know / no
knows / nose
lacks / lax
lain / lane
laps / lapse
larva / lava
lead / led
leak / leek
lessen / lesson
liar / lyre
licence / license
lieu / loo / Lou
lightening / lightning
links / lynx
load / lode
loan / lone
loot / lute
made / maid
mail / male
main / mane
maize / maze
mall / maul
manner / manor
mantel / mantle
mare / mayor
marshal / martial
meat / meet / mete
medal / meddle
metal / mettle
metre / meter
might / mite
mined / mind
miner / minor
missed / mist
moan / mown
moat / mote
mode / mowed
more / moor
morn / mourn
morning / mourning
muscle / mussel
mustard / mustered
nay / neigh
none / nun
ode / owed
one / won
paced / paste
packed / pact
pail / pale
pain / pane
pair / pare / pear
passed / past
patience / patients
paw / poor / pore
peace / piece
peak / peek
peer / pier
pedal / peddle

# WORD BANKS Prefixes

change word meaning

| a- *on, in, into, to* | ab- *off, away, from* | ad- *direction, addition* | after- *afterwards* | ante- *before in space/time* |
|---|---|---|---|---|
| aboard | abduct | adjacent | afterburner | antebellum |
| about | abhor | adjourn | afterimage | antecedent |
| adrift | abnormal | adjudicate | afterlife | antechamber |
| afoot | abort | adjust | aftermath | antedated |
| alight | absent | admire | afternoon | antelope |
| along | absolute | admit | aftershave | antemeridian |
| aloud | absolve | advance | aftershock | antemundane |
| among | absorb | advantage | aftertaste | antenatal |
| anew | abstain | adversity | afterthought | anterior |
| away | abstract | advocate | afterwards | anteroom |

| anti- *before in space/time* | arch- *first, chief* | auto- *self* | bene- *well* | bi- *two* |
|---|---|---|---|---|
| antibiotic | arch fiend | autobiography | benediction | bicentenary |
| anticlimax | arch rival | autocrat | benedictory | bicycle |
| anticlockwise | arch villain | autocue | benefaction | biennial |
| antidote | archangel | autograph | benefactor | bifocal |
| antifreeze | archbishop | autoharp | benefice | bilingual |
| antigovernment | archdeacon | automatic | beneficial | binoculars |
| antioxidant | archduchess | automaton | beneficiary | biped |
| antiperspirant | archduke | automobile | benefit | biplane |
| antisocial | archenemy | autopilot | benevolence | bipolar |
| antivenene | archetype | autosuggestion | benevolent | bisect |

| circum- *round* | co- *association/action* | com- *with, jointly* | con- *with, jointly, in combination* | contra- *opposite/opposing* |
|---|---|---|---|---|
| circumference | coagulate | combination | concentrate | contraband |
| circumfluent | coaxial | combine | condition | contrabass |
| circumlocutory | co-dependence | combustion | confide | contraception |
| circumnavigate | coerce | commence | congenial | contraceptive |
| circumscribe | coexist | commute | congratulate | contradict |
| circumspect | cohabit | complacent | connect | contralto |
| circumstance | cohesive | complain | consent | contravene |
| circumstantial | coincidence | complete | consider | |
| circumstantiate | cooperate | compose | converge | |
| circumvent | coordinate | compute | convince | |

# WORD BANKS Prefixes

**change word meaning**

| **counter-** *contrary to* | **de-** *separation, negation, reversal* | **di-** *through, between, across, by* | **dis-** *away, apart, reversing effect* | **down-** *downwards* |
|---|---|---|---|---|
| counteract | debrief | digest | disagree | downfall |
| counterattack | decay | digress | disappear | downgrade |
| counterbalance | decide | dilate | disband | downhearted |
| counterintelligence | decompose | dilute | discard | downhill |
| countermand | deduct | dimension | discourage | downpipe |
| counteroffensive | delay | direct | discover | downpour |
| counterpart | depend | divergent | dislocate | downstairs |
| countersign | destroy | divert | disobey | downstream |
| countersink | determine | divest | displace | downtown |
| counterweight | develop | divulge | dissolve | downtrodden |

| **dys-** *difficulty, poor condition* | **e-** *variant of ex-* | **en-** *in, into* | **epi-** *near, to, against, above, after, in addition to* | **eu-** *good, well* |
|---|---|---|---|---|
| dyscalculia | elaborate | enable | epicentre | eucalypt |
| dysentery | electric | enchant | epicure | Eucharist |
| dysfunctional | emerge | encircle | epidemic | euchre |
| dysgenic | enormous | encourage | epidermis | eulogy |
| dyslexia | eradicate | encroach | epigram | eunuch |
| dyspepsia | erase | enforce | epilogue | euphonium |
| dysphasia | erect | engulf | episode | eureka |
| dysphonic | evacuate | enlighten | epitaph | eurhythmic |
| dysphoria | evaluate | enliven | epithet | Europe |
| dysplasia | evolve | entreat | epitome | euthanasia |

| **ex-** *from, out of, utterly, thoroughly* | **extra-** *beyond, outside, besides* | **fore-** *front, ahead of time* | **hyper-** *over, excess, exaggeration* | **hypo-** *under, less, less than* |
|---|---|---|---|---|
| excavate | extradite | foreboding | hype | hypoactivity |
| exclaim | extragalactic | forecast | hyperactive | hypochondriac |
| exhale | extrajudicial | forefront | hyperbole | hypocrite |
| explain | extraneous | forego | hypermarket | hypocritical |
| explore | extraordinary | foreground | hyperphysical | hypodermic |
| export | extrapolate | forehead | hypersensitive | hypoglycaemia |
| ex-president | extrasensory | foreshadow | hypersonic | hypotenuse |
| exterminate | extraterrestrial | foretaste | hyperspace | hypothermia |
| extreme | extraterritorial | foretell | hypertension | hypothesis |
| ex-wife | extravagant | forewarn | hyperventilate | hypothetical |

# WORD BANKS Prefixes

## change word meaning

| **il-**<br>*variant of in-* | **im-**<br>*variant of in-* | **in-**<br>*not* | **inter-**<br>*between* | **mis-**<br>*mistaken, wrong, negation* |
|---|---|---|---|---|
| illegal | imbalance | inaccurate | interact | misbehave |
| illegible | immature | inanimate | interfere | miscalculate |
| illegitimate | immeasurable | inappropriate | interject | misfortune |
| illicit | immortal | inarticulate | intermingle | mishap |
| illiterate | immovable | incredible | international | misjudge |
| illogical | impassable | inexcusable | internet | misplace |
| ill-timed | impatient | inexplicable | interrupt | mispronounce |
| ill-treat | impersonal | informal | interschool | misrepresent |
| illuminate | impossible | invincible | intersect | mistrust |
| illustrious | improbable | invisible | interstate | misuse |

| **over-**<br>*above, beyond* | **para-**<br>*beyond, near, beside, amiss* | **peri-**<br>*around, about, beyond* | **post-**<br>*behind, after* | **pre-**<br>*before, prior to* |
|---|---|---|---|---|
| overall | parachute | perilous | postdate | precaution |
| overbearing | paradox | perimeter | posterity | precede |
| overboard | paragon | periodic | postgraduate | precooked |
| overdose | paragraph | peripatetic | posthumous | predict |
| overdue | parallel | peripheral | postmeridian pm | prefix |
| overhead | paramedic | periphery | post-mortem | prehistoric |
| overjoyed | paramount | periphrastic | postnatal | prejudge |
| overlook | paranormal | periscope | postpone | prelude |
| overrate | paraphernalia | peristyle | postposition | premonition |
| overtake | paraphrase | periwinkle | postscript | presuppose |

| **pro-**<br>*for, before, in favour of* | **re-**<br>*back, again, reversal* | **retro-**<br>*backwards in space and time* | **se-**<br>*setting apart, taking away* | **semi-**<br>*half* |
|---|---|---|---|---|
| probation | refer | retroactive | secede | semicircle |
| proceed | regain | retrocede | secluded | semicolon |
| profound | relate | retroflex | secrete | semiconscious |
| prognosis | relight | retrograde | secure | semidesert |
| program | remake | retrogressive | security | semidetached |
| progress | remit | retro-rocket | seduce | semifinal |
| prohibit | replay | retrorse | select | semiprecious |
| prologue | restore | retrospect | semester | semiquaver |
| promote | resume | retrospective | sequence | semiskilled |
| pronounce | return | retroversion | serene | semitone |

# WORD BANKS Prefixes

## change word meaning

| sub- *under, not quite* | super- *above, superior* | sym- *variant of syn-* | syn- *association (like co-)* | trans- *across, beyond* |
|---|---|---|---|---|
| subcontract | supercharged | symbol | synagogue | transcontinental |
| subheading | superimpose | symbolic | synapsis | transfer |
| submerge | superintendent | symmetrical | synchronise | transform |
| subsonic | supermarket | symmetry | synchronous | translate |
| substandard | supernatural | sympathise | syndicate | translucent |
| substitute | supersede | sympathy | syndrome | transmit |
| subterranean | superstar | symphony | synergy | transparent |
| subtitle | superstructure | symphysis | syntax | transport |
| subtropical | super-tanker | symposium | synthesis | transpose |
| subway | supervise | symptom | synthesise | transverse |

| tri- *three* | ultra- *beyond in space and time* | un- *not, opposite to, reversal of state* | under- *below – place or situation* | up- *upwards* |
|---|---|---|---|---|
| triangle | ultra sensitive | unarmed | underclothes | update |
| triceps | ultraconservative | unbeatable | underdog | upgrade |
| tricolour | ultracritical | unbend | underestimate | upheaval |
| tricycle | ultrafilter | unclean | undergrowth | uphill |
| triennial | ultraloyal | undesirable | underline | uplifted |
| trihedron | ultramarine | unfold | undermine | up-market |
| trilogy | ultraradical | untimely | underneath | upright |
| trimaran | ultrasonic | untraceable | undernourished | upstage |
| triplets | ultrasound | untruth | undervalue | upstart |
| tripod | ultraviolet | unusual | underweight | upstream |

## Adjective-forming suffixes

| -al | -ive | -ish | -ic | -ent |
|---|---|---|---|---|
| casual<br>coastal<br>lethal<br>local<br>minimal<br>occasional<br>personal<br>regional<br>thermal<br>usual | active<br>attentive<br>attractive<br>compulsive<br>effective<br>festive<br>impulsive<br>negative<br>positive<br>sensitive | babyish<br>brownish<br>devilish<br>foolish<br>impish<br>oldish<br>peckish<br>Spanish<br>stylish<br>sweetish | bombastic<br>comic<br>domestic<br>dramatic<br>idiotic<br>optimistic<br>pessimistic<br>rustic<br>static<br>toxic | deficient<br>dependent<br>despondent<br>efficient<br>eloquent<br>insolent<br>proficient<br>prominent<br>reverent<br>transient |
| **-ful** | **-less** | **-some** | **-able** | **-ible** |
| careful<br>cheerful<br>colourful<br>doubtful<br>fanciful<br>helpful<br>peaceful<br>powerful<br>thoughtful<br>truthful | breathless<br>defenceless<br>fearless<br>leaderless<br>merciless<br>motherless<br>numberless<br>relentless<br>sleepless<br>timeless | awesome<br>bothersome<br>cumbersome<br>flavoursome<br>gruesome<br>handsome<br>loathsome<br>meddlesome<br>tiresome<br>wearisome | agreeable<br>changeable<br>comfortable<br>desirable<br>fashionable<br>miserable<br>reasonable<br>reliable<br>untraceable<br>workable | admissible<br>divisible<br>edible<br>horrible<br>in/visible<br>incredible<br>possible<br>responsible<br>sensible<br>terrible |
| **-er -est**<br>*comparative/superlative* | **-ial** | **-ous** | **-ious** | **y-** |
| calmer calmest<br>faster fastest<br>happier happiest<br>higher highest<br>hotter hottest<br>longer longest<br>older oldest<br>slower slowest<br>thicker thickest<br>thinner thinnest | beneficial<br>commercial<br>differential<br>influential<br>official<br>partial<br>preferential<br>sequential<br>superficial<br>territorial | adventurous<br>continuous<br>famous<br>generous<br>jealous<br>mountainous<br>nervous<br>perilous<br>pompous<br>venomous | delicious<br>devious<br>fallacious<br>gracious<br>illustrious<br>impervious<br>malicious<br>officious<br>precious<br>spacious | fizzy<br>funny<br>greasy<br>greedy<br>hungry<br>risky<br>speedy<br>sunny<br>tasty<br>tricky |

# WORD BANKS Suffixes

## change word grammar

### Noun-forming suffixes

| -acy | -ant | -ary -ory -ery | -ance | -ence |
|---|---|---|---|---|
| accuracy | assistant | cemetery | abundance | competence |
| bureaucracy | attendant | diary | accordance | conference |
| conspiracy | combatant | dispensary | circumstance | correspondence |
| democracy | commandant | documentary | distance | dependence |
| fallacy | confidant | eatery | disturbance | eloquence |
| intimacy | consonant | factory | elegance | experience |
| legacy | dependant | infirmary | entrance | inference |
| lunacy | pedant | mortuary | nuisance | innocence |
| piracy | pendant | refectory | performance | persistence |
| privacy | servant | seminary | reluctance | pretence |

| -ium | -er | -ism | -ist | -ice |
|---|---|---|---|---|
| aquarium | announcer | communism | dentist | apprentice |
| auditorium | baker | escapism | egotist | armistice |
| conservatorium | builder | fanaticism | exhibitionist | cornice |
| millennium | buyer | fatalism | extremist | in/justice |
| planetarium | cricketer | favouritism | guitarist | novice |
| podium | dancer | idealism | opportunist | police |
| premium | driver | impressionism | racist | practice |
| solarium | photographer | racism | sadist | prejudice |
| stadium | teacher | rheumatism | soloist | service |
| terrarium | trader | unionism | violinistaccomplice | |

| -cle | -hood | -itis | -ion | -tion |
|---|---|---|---|---|
| debacle | adulthood | appendicitis | apprehension | collection |
| icicle | babyhood | arthritis | conclusion | competition |
| manacle | brotherhood | bronchitis | decision | destination |
| monocle | childhood | dermatitis | derision | education |
| oracle | falsehood | fibrositis | illusion | pollution |
| particle | fatherhood | laryngitis | impression | explanation |
| pinnacle | motherhood | meningitis | occasion | illustration |
| receptacle | parenthood | peritonitis | opinion | instruction |
| spectacle | priesthood | sinusitis | pension | invitation |
| tentacle | sainthood | tonsillitis | question | recreation |

# WORD BANKS Suffixes change word grammar

## Noun-forming suffixes

| -ment | -ness | -ship | -ity | -ian |
|---|---|---|---|---|
| amazement | awkwardness | censorship | authenticity | electrician |
| amusement | carelessness | companionship | complicity | guardian |
| appointment | darkness | craftsmanship | domesticity | Italian |
| engagement | laziness | fellowship | electricity | mathematician |
| entertainment | madness | friendship | facility | musician |
| management | selfishness | horsemanship | familiarity | paediatrician |
| movement | softness | leadership | mediocrity | pedestrian |
| predicament | sweetness | partnership | security | politician |
| refreshment | tenderness | relationship | similarity | technician |
| wonderment | uneasiness | scholarship | toxicity | vegetarian |
| **-age** | **-ent -ee** | **-le** | **-or** | **-ette** |
| blockage | agent | battle | actor | cigarette |
| bondage | antecedent | bubble | author | dinette |
| breakage | devotee | bundle | conductor | diskette |
| damage | employee | candle | contractor | etiquette |
| foliage | evacuee | couple | doctor | kitchenette |
| hostage | precedent | kettle | mentor | marionette |
| leakage | president | pimple | sailor | rosette |
| marriage | refugee | puzzle | sculptor | silhouette |
| postage | respondent | rifle | senator | suffragette |
| storage | student | saddle | visitor | usherette |

## Adverb-forming suffixes

| -ly | -ward/s | -wise | -way/s |
|---|---|---|---|
| busily | afterward | anticlockwise | always |
| daily | backwards | clockwise | anyway |
| gladly | downwards | crosswise | away |
| honestly | forwards | lengthwise | everyway |
| lately | homeward | likewise | lengthways |
| presently | inwards | moneywise | longways |
| quietly | outwards | otherwise | sideways |
| reluctantly | towards | pennywise | someway |
| slowly | wayward | timewise | underway |
| usually | westward | waterwise | |